Worthy

*The true story of an abused child's struggle
for survival and acceptance*

By Kimberly Plante

Published by RebelBooksPress.com
A division of The Jersey Tomato Press, LLC

ISBN: 979-8-9869393-0-8

Published in the United States by RebelBooksPress.com

Editor: Sarah E. Anderson

Front and back cover design by Sarah E. Anderson

Manufactured in the United States

First Edition

To my children — Jessica, Justin, Jordan, Colin, Jake, and Julia. I love you all so very much, more than anything — more than everything.

Preface

December 27, 2019: My husband and I were at Newark airport. Our flight was delayed again. After killing time eating an overpriced dinner, we were on the hunt for a couple of seats at the gate to wait it out. Tim could tell that I was emotionally drained, my head still trying to process what had just happened over the last few days, dreading the fact that we were leaving. The last thing I wanted to do was engage in small talk, and he respected this, so we walked to our gate in silence. The airport was overcrowded with holiday travelers, but he somehow spotted two empty seats at a table with four grimy tablets secured to the tabletop for ordering food. He made a beeline toward the table, yelling over his shoulder for me to hurry up.

I plopped my bag on the floor next to me and sat down on a bar-height chair that was bolted to the floor. A couple sat across the table from us. She looked to be in her mid-sixties and had a kind face and tired eyes. She was wearing a nasal cannula and using oxygen. I wanted to ask why but didn't. A half-drank bottle of Diet Coke sat in front of her, and she looked at me and smiled. Her husband, a stocky, stoic man, sat next to her, looking a little bored. I asked where they were flying to. They were on the same flight as us, which made me happy. She seemed so familiar though I was sure we had never met before. She and her husband were from South Dakota and had the dialect to prove it. I loved how she would say "Ya know" as we chatted.

After our small talk about travel (because that's what traveling strangers do) and the holidays, the conversation turned to why my husband and I were so far away from home. Naomi (that was her name) shared that their family had   spent Christmas together, singing carols and touring New York City. Both her daughters lived on the East Coast and had hosted all 17 family members. She proudly pulled out her phone and showed me photos full of smiling faces of all ages, and I could tell that they all had a wonderful time. She was uniquely personable and authentic, and something about her drew me to her and made me feel connected in a very unexpected way.

I loved listening to her tell me about her family Christmas, but suddenly I found myself growing so anxious to tell my story that I could hardly sit still. When the conversation turned toward me, I shared that we had six grown children. I could tell she thought it odd we weren't home spending Christmas with them because she asked why we were on the East Coast when none of our kids lived there. It was exactly the question I had been waiting for.

"Is it a large family?" she asked.

"Yes," I said. "And I just met them."

The look on Naomi's face was one I will never forget. By now, she was standing up. Her eyes were filled with curiosity and intrigue. She grabbed my hand and said, "I have to go to the ladies' room, but when I get back, I want to hear every word."

Part 1

Chapter 1

Despite everything, I have always known what love feels like. Some of my dearest and earliest memories are of my grandfather. A loving and sweet man, he would sit me on his lap and always have M&M's for me. My last memory I have of him is when I was about two and a half. I remember going to visit him at a hospital. I was so excited to see him because I knew he would give me M&M's. This visit was different from the others, though. This time, his room was dark when Gram and I walked in the door, and he had his eyes closed. He was lying still like he was asleep. I remember running up to his bed and climbing up to sit beside him, just as I had the other times we came to visit. But this time, as I crawled up to sit by him, he screamed in pain and pushed me away. His reaction scared me.

"I'm sorry, I'm sorry," I said over and over.

Gram quickly snatched me off the bed and sat me in a chair. As she spoke to Papa, I could hear pain and anger in his voice, something I had never heard from him before. It was time to leave. Gram took my hand and led me to the door. As we left, I said, "Bye, Papa," too afraid to turn and see his face. But right before we reached the door, he called me over to him. I let go of Gram's hand and ran back. He reached his arms out to give me a hug. Although I was reluctant to touch him and didn't want to make him yell in pain again, I needed his hug. He was so different this time, and I was afraid. Carefully, I crawled onto his bed and let him wrap his arms around me. I was right where I belonged. The hug was soft, and I could hear his breathing as I lay my head on his frail chest. After a few seconds, Gram once again took my hand, and it was time to go. As we were walking away, he reached into the drawer next to him and pulled out a bag of M&M's. He said, "Kimmy, don't forget your treat," I went back to his side, and he placed the entire bag in my hand. I usually got just four or five, never the whole bag. This was different. Especially since I had hurt him. But he wasn't angry with me. In fact, he wanted to make sure I knew this with his soft hug and extra special treat.

As we walked away, he said, "Goodbye, Kimmy. I love you."

"I love you, too, Papa."

That was the last time Gram and I visited the hospital and the last special treat or soft hug my Papa gave to me.

I didn't really understand why we never went back to see him, and when I asked, Gram just said, "Papa is in a better place now."

In 1969, I was three years old, and I lived with Gram in the home built by Papa. It was a red, brick, Cape-style home. Gram's room was upstairs, and I slept in there with her. Her room had a floral print wallpaper and a large bed with a white chenille bedspread. Delicate pine cones were carved into the bedpost. The morning sun would shine into the front windows illuminating the dust that danced in the air. Her room had an old Singer sewing machine, at which she would sit for hours during the day. A soft, multicolored afghan that she made lay across the foot of her bed. This was my special blanket. Every night, I would lie next to her under this blanket, and she would say the Lord's Prayer with me. The room was always so dark when we said this prayer, but she would take my hand and gently squeeze it, just to let me know she was there.

Gram was a tall woman with broad shoulders and short, gray, curly hair. She had a strong face with thin lips. Her eyes conveyed a life of struggle, and the chip in her front tooth confirmed it. She didn't hug me much but did tell me she loved me occasionally. Sometimes, she would say, "When your mother comes back, she will take care of you." I wasn't sure who she was talking about. *Gram was my mother*, I thought.

Why didn't she want to be my mom? There was a picture of my real mother hanging downstairs on the wall by our tan, rotary-dial phone, but that was just a faded photo — not a real person.

Days at Gram's were mostly happy. I'd busy myself doing things toddlers do. One of my favorite pastimes was sliding down the dark-teal, shag-carpeted stairs on my bum. I'd sit at the top and open my mouth, so as my bum bounced off each step, I let out a reverberating, silly sound. If I got caught, though, Gram would scold me and tell me to stop. It was midway down a forbidden ride one day when the front door opened, and the person in the faded photo entered the house.

Her face was crooked, and the corners of her mouth pulled her cheeks and eyes into a scowl, as though she were perpetually angry. I wondered if this was what Gram meant when she sometimes told me my face would get stuck like that if I didn't turn my frown upside down. Her eyes darted around the room intentionally, as though she were simultaneously looking for something while hating everything she saw. She had blonde hair pulled back and teased high on her head. She stank of cigarettes. She wore a light-blue button-down shirt that was snug across her middle and hung over her tan pedal-pushers. She didn't smile, and she didn't look at me. There was nothing warm or inviting about her. Behind her was a man with very short, jet-black hair. He had olive skin and wore a white t-shirt with the short sleeves rolled up. He had a nice smile, but like her, he was a stranger to me.

I felt uncomfortable and immediately stopped playing as I called out for Gram.

The strange man walked toward me and said, "You must be Kim," as my mother walked past me toward the kitchen, without even looking up at me. I was surprised he knew my name and wondered why it was him talking to me and not my mother. I sat mid-stair, wondering what she was doing here, why she came back, and thinking that neither of them belonged in my home.

10

Chapter 2

This stranger that showed up that day seemed to think she was in charge of me.

"Kim," she said. "Time to turn off the TV."

I obeyed but wondered where Gram was. At dinnertime, she told me to come to the table, and then she set a plate in front of me. I sat at the table alone and wasn't sure what everyone else was doing. At bedtime, this woman opened the door to the bedroom off the kitchen and said, "It's time for bed."

I don't know why I didn't try to explain that I slept upstairs with Gram. She didn't seem like a woman I should argue with. So I went into the large room and crawled into the twin bed with a high wooden headboard and pulled the dark blue blanket up to my chin. It smelled like mothballs. She turned out the light, and for the first time, I was alone in the dark. No prayers. No holding Gram's hand. No, "I love you." No hugs or kisses.

To my disappointment, the two strangers didn't leave. In fact, they were always around. Mom and Ritchie were at Gram's when I woke up each morning and when I went to bed each night. The house seemed very different. Gram seemed different. The special nightly prayers were over, and I had to keep sleeping by myself. I missed Gram and didn't understand why things had changed. The closeness Gram and I shared had changed, and she seemed more distant. Instead of eating scrambled eggs and toast or biscuits and gravy with Gram, I ate cereal by myself. I was used to Gram reading me devotionals during breakfast, but with Mom and Ritchie there, they talked among themselves about grown-up things. I was expected to sit quietly. Over the next few days and weeks, I adjusted to them being around, learning to play quietly in a closet that doubled as a pass-through between my new bedroom and the living room.

A few weeks later, Ritchie and Mom, as I had come to call them, were married, and the three of us moved into a very small house in Monroe, Connecticut. I liked the idea of being part of a family, and I was excited about this new adventure. They let me pick out the paint color for my new bedroom and installed new flooring. I chose pink for the walls and Flower Power linoleum with yellow, green, and pink flowers for the floor. It wasn't far from Gram's house, and everyone seemed to be in a happy place.

Ritchie often played with me and made me feel special. The small house had a standalone garage, where Ritchie had tools and worked on things that produced tiny metal shavings in sparkly spirals that littered the floor and glistened if the light caught them just right. I loved being with him in the musty shed, watching him build or fix things inside. He would lift me up onto his counter and ask me to help by holding a screwdriver or some bolts. Together we assembled a TV stand, and it was my job to make sure none of the hardware fell on the floor.

As long as he was home, Mom was nice. We all ate dinner together, and after dinner, we'd watch *I Love Lucy*. One morning, after I had started to feel settled in my new life, I woke up in a wet bed. My footie pajamas (with the feet cut off, so I could grow) were soaked. This had happened before, and when it did, Gram would put me in the tub, dress me in dry clothes, change my sheets, and remind me, "No drinks after dinner." I slid off my bed and went to find Mom. She was still in bed, sound asleep.

"Mom," I said as I approached her bed. "I had an accident."

She took a second to open her eyes. She reached her hand out to feel my pajamas.

"What the fuck?!" she scolded. Her eyes turned mean, and I felt like they were trying to drill a hole into my face.

I was stunned. It seemed like a switch had flipped in her.

"Why didn't you get up if you had to pee?" she yelled. She stormed into my room and pointed to my bed. "Now you're going to have to sleep in these sheets."

"I didn't mean to. I'm sorry," I cried.

She stormed off and left me standing in wet pajamas, alone with tears running down my face. She didn't wash the sheets. She didn't bathe me or change me out of my pajamas. I missed Gram.

At nap time, she marched me into my bedroom.

"This is what you get for peeing the bed like a baby," she said.

I crawled into bed. It smelled bad. I was used to Gram's perfume, but this smelled horrible, rancid. I wondered why she was being so mean to me. I thought about how Gram had always told me that I didn't belong with her because she wasn't my mother. But now I was with my mother, and all I could think was, "I don't belong here."

I had hoped that day was just a bad day, but instead, it became a new normal. When Ritchie was at work, Mom yelled at me a lot. She called me a baby and sent me to my room often. I felt like I was always in her way and spent my time trying to be good and quiet... I tried to be invisible. I stayed in my room alone, quietly busying myself with Tinker Toys or coloring.

In the evenings, not long after the sun went down, I'd listen for Ritchie's car door, which was my sign that I could leave my room and be a part of the family. He'd walk through the front door as I walked out of my bedroom, and he would pick me up and give me a big hug. I'd wrap my arms around him, so happy he was home.

About a year later, when I was four, my brother, David, arrived. My mother would kiss him and hold him and speak softly to him. She fussed over him, making sure he was warm enough, his tummy was full, and his diaper was dry. She used a baby voice with him and tended to him every time he cried. It was a side of her I hadn't seen before.

Ritchie was also sweet with the baby. Instead of taking me into the tool shed, Ritchie would play with David. He'd lay on the living room floor with the baby and make him laugh and smile. As David grew a little older, Ritchie would throw him into the air, and David would squeal with delight. I'd stand in the doorway between my room and the living room, watching, feeling sad and left out.

Mom didn't even pretend to care about me. I was in her way, a nuisance. I could sense she didn't want me around and that she'd rather spend time with David. I tried to find ways to get her attention. With Gram, I'd pick a dandelion and give it to her. Gram would say, "This is the most beautiful flower anyone has ever picked for me," and put it in water in a tiny jar and save it until it died.

One day, I tried this with Mom. "That's a weed," Mom said, and threw it in the trash. She turned her back to me and continued tending to David.

I wondered if there was something wrong with me. She was my mom, and she was supposed to save it in a jar in the window like Gram did.

Most days, I ate toast and poached eggs with Ritchie before he left for work. He always left when it was dark outside, but I made sure I was up in time to see him. Hours later, when Mom woke up, she'd have a cigarette and take David out of his crib. Sometimes, I would ask to watch TV or play outside, but even if I didn't ask, she told me to clean my room. I'd walk in and hear her lock the door behind me. I stayed there until just before Ritchie came home. Sometimes she would let me out to use the bathroom, but mostly she didn't. I sat against my door, begging her to open it.

"I'm hungry, and I have to go potty," I cried. "Please open the door, Mommy! I promise to be a good girl if you unlock the door." In the beginning, if I cried long enough, she would open the door and beat me for crying. The washer and dryer sat in the hallway outside of my room, and she kept a belt on top of the dryer. She grabbed me by the hair, pulled my pants down, and whipped me on my bottom with the belt.

While she did this, I always wet myself, so then she would whip me for that, too. Afterward, she'd put me right back in my room and lock the door. Eventually, she stopped opening it altogether. As awful as that was, the worst part was that she would tell Ritchie.

"Kim peed her pants like a baby," she said one night.

I felt my cheeks go hot. I looked at Ritchie to see how he'd respond. I was so scared he would be mad at me and not love me anymore.

"That's okay, Kim," he said. "Just try not to wait too long if you have to use the bathroom."

A wave of relief washed over me. He knew I wasn't a baby. He knew I didn't do it on purpose. I wanted to tell him why it happened, but even at four and a half, I knew better.

Chapter 3

My kindergarten year is a blur to me except for three things: a dead moose that hung in a large tree on our side yard for weeks; being so happy to be out of my room and out of the house Monday through Friday, and making butter with my classmates.

Ritchie was Native American and loved to hunt — and we needed the meat. He shot the moose with his friend Bill and hung it in the tree to cure. I felt sad for the moose, and I also felt embarrassed because it was ugly and gross. Other kids got their food from the grocery store. They didn't hang it from trees and cut it up in the backyard and fill a freezer with it. I was nervous to eat it, too. I didn't know what it would taste like, but I knew it wasn't hamburger.

Our house was the closest one on the bus route to the school, so I was the last to get picked up in the morning and the first to get off in the afternoon. Kindergarten was only half a day, so I came home around noon. When I got home, Mom would be sitting on the porch, smoking a cigarette, and then would send me straight to my room. I stayed there until Ritchie got home, which got later and later as the year went on, making my days longer and longer. The good news was that she didn't lock the door anymore, and I could use the bathroom when I needed to. By the end of the year, he didn't get home until after bedtime, which meant I didn't get lunch or dinner. I'd lie in bed at night looking forward to my poached eggs and toast with Ritchie in the morning while I listened to my stomach growl.

One day, my kindergarten teacher, Mrs. Dorian, told all the boys and girls to get in a circle. She filled a big Mason jar with cream and asked us to pass it around the circle. Each of us would take turns shaking the jar ten times before passing it on to the next person. The

16

jar went around the circle many times, and every time it got to me, the cream was a little thicker. I didn't know what was happening, but the cream was transforming before my eyes. When the cream became solid, she had us line up and gave us each two saltine crackers. When I got to the front of the line, she used a knife to spread the cream onto my crackers. I took a bite. It was butter! And it was delicious. As I sat with my saltines and apple juice, I was amazed and enthralled with what we had done.

On the bus ride home, I was still in awe of how we turned simple cream into butter. It seemed like magic, and I was sure that we were the first kids to discover it. For the first time in my life, I felt proud of something I had done, and I wore that pride like a cape.

When I got home, Mom was having a cigarette on the porch, like usual. I was so excited to tell someone of our discovery.

"Mom, guess what I did today?" I asked excitedly. She looked at me and raised her eyebrows. "Mrs. Dorian put milk in a jar, and we shook it and shook it, and it turned into butter! And we put it on saltines, and it was amazing! We did it all by ourselves."

I hadn't really thought through how I expected her to respond. I just couldn't contain my excitement.

"How stupid are you?" she replied. "Butter is made from cream. There was nothing magical about what you did. All you did was shake a jar."

My heart sank. I really thought we had done something special. I picked up my backpack and walked to my room. Getting off the bus, I felt like I had invented butter, and minutes later, I felt stupid and embarrassed. My heart sank when she said those words, and I was pulled back into feeling like no matter what I did, I failed.

When Kindergarten had started I was excited. Gram had made me some new clothes that made me feel pretty. They weren't like my old clothes that reeked of pee. She made me a pretty dress that was white with red polka dots and had a ruffle at the bottom with a sash that tied at my waist behind me. That was my favorite, but it, too, became just like the rest after a while.

I did the best that I could trying to take care of myself. I was allowed to bathe on Saturday or Sunday (but never both days on the same weekend), probably because Ritchie was home. He had bought me a box of Mr. Bubble one day in the fall when we went to the IGA for groceries. It came in a white cardboard box, with a cartoon picture of a bubble guy smiling in the tub and lots of bubbles surrounding him; it had a metal spout on the side. I was so excited that I didn't even put the box in the shopping cart. I just carried it proudly through the store aisles.

"Now, Kim," he said as we checked out. "You can't use a lot. Just a little bit goes a long way."

Once we got home, I was super careful to sprinkle just enough, counting to three, as the light, pink powder fell into the old bathtub with the stained, brown ring halfway up and a washcloth stuffed into the drain to stop the water from escaping. I would sit in my bubbles until the water became too cool and my fingers were wrinkled like prunes. Sometimes my pajamas were clean, but most times, they weren't. The sweet fragrance from my bubbles rose above even the pee odor. The light, bubbly smell reminded me of Gram's room. After these bubble baths, I would lie in bed when the room was dark and say the special prayer Gram and I shared, wishing she were beside me again.

Ritchie also bought me my first box of new Crayola crayons that day. I had no idea how exciting a new box of crayons was until I opened them. They were perfect. All the colors lined up straight in the yellow and green box. Sixty-four new, beautiful crayons and, like my bubbles, had a smell unique and glorious all their own. They were perfect, not one broken, each having a place, standing tall and proud. The only other crayons I had had before were broken, and I guess that's what I expected when I opened this box, too, none being more than one or two inches long, with their outside paper jackets peeled off. My old crayons lived in an old rusty coffee can and had since the day I got them.

Ritchie made most days better — even his punishments were better. One day, he came home from the barber smelling so good, and his hair was so short that when he let me rub the top of his head, it tickled my hand.

"It's a crew cut," he said. "Do you like it?"

His hair was always cut short, jet black, and slicked back. With a buzz cut, he looked so handsome, and I hugged him as I rubbed the top of his head. I never answered his question. I just embraced his strong hug, my hand still feeling the top of his head, as I buried my face in his shoulder.

The next day, we went to Gram's, and as I ran through the door, I was welcomed by the familiar smells and the same teal-green carpet. My aunt Sandy and cousin Kelly were often at Gram's visiting. Kelly and I were 18 months apart, her being the younger of us. I watched the interaction between Sandy and Kelly and knew it was something I didn't have. On the few occasions Sandy left Kelly for a few hours at Gram's, Sandy always came back, and there were always hugs and kisses when she left and when she returned. My aunt would ask, "How was your day, Princess?" or "What did you do today?"

"I drew a picture," Kelly would reply, and then Aunt Sandy would take the colored piece of paper with scribbled flowers and a house drawn between them, smile and hug her, and say, "This is the most beautiful picture I've ever seen."

They hugged and said "I love you" to each other every day. And when Kelly had an accident, Aunt Sandy never put her in a room for the day with no food or water. Instead, she washed and changed Kelly's clothes and put on a clean pair of pretty panties that had ruffles on the bum. If they stayed the night, my aunt would make sure Kelly had Captain Crunch cereal, the red box, her favorite, waiting for her in the morning when she woke up.

I would watch my aunt help Kelly dress in the morning. Clean, pretty clothes, and she would sit and brush her long, beautiful hair. When she was done, she'd kiss Kelly on the top of her head and say, "Okay, Princess. Time for breakfast." My hair was a short tousled mess, and no one brushed it for me. I wanted someone to. And I wanted someone to call me "princess." I didn't ask Aunt Sandy to brush my hair, though, because I felt like I didn't belong in their special group. I was an outsider just watching how a mom loves her child, wishing someone loved me like that.

Despite the clear inequities in our mothers' treatment of us, I loved playing with Kelly. It was one of the only times I got to play with another child. So that day, when we arrived, Kelly came out of the kitchen, and off we went — cousins off to the back room to hide and play while the grown-ups went to the kitchen to get ready for dinner. After dinner, Kelly and I went back to playing, and I came up with a great idea.

"Let's play barber!" I said. We ran upstairs to find Gram's metal scissors with the broken tip on her sewing table. My hair was already very short, but Kelly had long, beautiful blonde hair, so we both agreed that I would be the barber and she the customer. As I cut her hair, I thought I was doing a great job. When I was done, we ran to the bathroom to look at her new 'do, and she started to cry.

"Please don't cry," I kept saying. Aunt Sandy must have heard her crying and found us in the bathroom. Kelly was still crying when Aunt Sandy grabbed my arm and pulled me into the kitchen, where all the adults were having coffee.

"Look!" she screamed, as Kelly stood behind her, her hair now lopsided and as short as mine.

"Look what Kim did!" she yelled at my mom and Ritchie — mostly Ritchie, though, like it was his fault, expecting him to punish me. I was confused as to what I did wrong and scared because my mother was glaring at me from across the table with a stare I knew all too well, terrified of what she was going to do.

Instead, it was Ritchie who took over.

"I'll take care of it," he said. "Back off, Sandy."

But Sandy was very demanding.

"Well, aren't you going to spank her?" Sandy yelled. "Look what she did!"

Ritchie ignored her and told Mom it was time to go.

The ride home was filled with arguing. Mom didn't take my side; she said that I was the instigator. Ritchie argued the opposite, and my heart raced. I sat staring out the window, wishing I weren't there. *What was he thinking?* I kept wondering. *What did I do wrong?* I asked myself. *I just gave her a haircut. What's an instigator?* All of these thoughts and questions played through my mind.

We pulled into the driveway, and Mom got out of the car, slamming her door behind her. Ritchie sat there for a minute. I could see his face in the rearview mirror. He caught me looking at him, got out of the car, and opened my door silently.

I got out and followed behind him as he walked into the house. Again, Mom started yelling at him for not handling the situation. I just stood there like I was invisible, waiting for my punishment from her. But it was Ritchie who delivered it, and it shook me.

"Go to your room, Kim. Now!" he yelled. This time I went to my room, and I didn't beg to get out. I felt like, somehow, I deserved it, and I hoped Ritchie wouldn't hate me for doing something wrong. I lay on my pillow, crying, begging God for forgiveness, and for Ritchie to still love me even though I was bad.

When I woke early the next morning, my room was still dark, but I could smell coffee, which meant Ritchie was up. I sat on the side of the bed, afraid to go out where he was, but I had to use the potty, so, quietly, I opened my door and tiptoed to the bathroom, which was to the right of my room. I didn't turn the light on, and I made it through the dark to the toilet, not flushing when I was done, just to be quiet.

When I opened the bathroom door, he was standing a few feet in front of me. I stopped dead in my tracks, quickly looking away, afraid to see the same angry face from last night. He was quiet for a few seconds, and then I felt his hand on my shoulder. It was soft and warm, and immediately, I started crying and begging for his forgiveness.

"I am so sorry I was a bad girl. I won't do it again. I promise." I said.

He knelt down and wrapped his arms around me in the best hug.

"*Underdog* is on, and breakfast is ready," he said. "How about me and my special girl go eat before it's cold?"

And just like that, what happened the night before was forgiven. He didn't hate me, and I was happy.

Chapter 4

I spent much of my first-grade year confused about a number of things. For instance, Gram was a Jehovah's Witness, so we didn't celebrate birthdays or Christmas, which meant I never received actual presents. But one time, a week before first grade was set to start, Ritchie came home from work with a new *Flintstones* lunch box. I was so excited. I loved *The Flintstones* almost as much as *Underdog*, but mostly I'd never been given a surprise gift before. The notion that Ritchie — or anyone for that matter — would take the time to think about what I liked and buy it for me as a surprise, just to make me happy... It made me feel like the most special person in the world.

Even though being Jehovah's Witness meant no presents, Christmas, or birthdays, other rules seemed optional. Mom and Ritchie never took me to the Kingdom Hall. And they both smoked and drank, which is forbidden, so I didn't understand why we couldn't have a Christmas tree or birthday party. Ritchie drank way more than she did, and they fought a lot about his drinking. He and Mom sometimes fought before David was born. They would yell at each other, and then he would go outside to the work shed and smoke a cigarette or pipe. Once my brother arrived, they fought much more. Ritchie rarely came home before I went to bed. I'd lie awake listening for his car to pull up, hoping he would stay. I listened as Mom called everyone she knew to find him.

When he was home, they argued about him drinking his paycheck away and swearing they never wanted to see each other again. As the fights got worse, he came home less and less. I blamed Mom; she yelled and screamed all the time. I wished he would come and take me with him. The fighting, him not coming home, and her calling to try and find him became the norm — until October 12, 1972.

It started as a normal day and a predictable night. Another fight between my parents in the morning, complete with swearing, yelling, and threats of divorce. Then I heard doors slam and his car peel away from the house. I didn't get dinner and was sent to bed early, which was not unusual. As I lay in bed, I could hear her calling around again, trying to find him. A few hours later, I awoke to a banging on the front door. It was raining so hard that it pounded on my windows, and I couldn't see who was at the front door.

Afraid, I jumped from my bed and peeked from my bedroom door to see who it was, thinking that Ritchie had probably got locked out again. Instead, I saw my mother standing with the front door half open, speaking to two police officers. Rain ran over the brims of their black hats, and their badges shone on their jackets. This startled me. I thought maybe she'd made good on one of her many promises to call the police on me for backtalk or some other offense like peeing my pants or cutting Kelly's hair.

She was calm as she spoke to them, her voice quiet. The bright light that illuminated the front stoop made it very easy to see her face and the faces of our midnight visitors — even through the rain. She didn't appear mad and had not invited them in to take me away, so I stepped out from behind the cracked door and asked her who was here. She immediately whipped her head around and yelled, "Get your ass back in bed, and if I see you up, you will get the belt."

This was a phrase I knew well, so I put the policemen out of my head and ran back to my warm, safe bed, grateful to have avoided the belt, and fell back to sleep.

"Where's Ritchie?" I asked Mom in the morning.

"He was in a car accident and is at the hospital, but he'll be home soon," She said. "You're not going to school today. We're going to Gram's."

Yes! I thought. *Today is going to be great!*

I knew Aunt Sandy and Kelly would be there because they were living with Gram now, so I got dressed at lightning speed, hoping that there would be breakfast because I was starving. Mom was quiet as we drove to Gram's house, except for the two times she yelled at David, who had started to cry halfway there. He was still in his pajamas from the night before and smelled of a dirty diaper. After the second "Shut the hell up!" from the front seat, I dug into the diaper bag, found his bottle, and gave it to him. He stopped crying, and we made our way to Gram's in stinky silence.

Usually, when we rode in the car, she'd have the radio turned up high with the window open, so she could flick her cigarette ashes into the wind — even in the dead of winter. But not on this ride. No music, no window open, with smoke and ashes filling the car. Her demeanor made me very uncomfortable. I stared out my window, counting the telephone poles. When we turned down Gram's street, I was relieved that it was almost over. Gram lived at the bottom of a hill on a dead-end street. Mom parked the car, swooped up my brother, and walked toward the house, not saying a word to me. I grabbed the paper bag that carried the diapers for David and followed her inside. She had left the front door open, and once I walked in, I quickly shut it. Gram had a strict rule about keeping the doors shut and not wasting heat. Hoping she hadn't seen the door left open, I put the bag down and walked into the living room, where Kelly was lying on the floor watching cartoons.

Gram had a big console TV, which hadn't worked for as long as I could remember. On top of it was a much smaller TV with two silver antennae with aluminum foil balled up on each end. It was prehistoric and black-and-white, but it worked. As I walked toward the center of the living room, tiny particles of dust floated like little flecks of gold. The sun was rising, and the rays came into the front window illuminating the dust and filling the room with a warm light. *Underdog* was on the screen, and I was thrilled.

"Hi," I said, as I sat to watch the show on the carpet beside her.

Kelly turned on her side to greet me. "Now you and I are the same."

The same, I thought. *Not possible.*

She was very pretty and petite and had a really cool mom that liked her and didn't use the belt or say mean things like my mother did. *Nope,* I thought. *You are wrong. We are nothing alike.* But she then added, "Now you don't have a daddy, either."

Her mom was a single mother, and Kelly grew up never knowing her father. I instantly replied, "Yes, I do. I have my stepdad."

"Not anymore. He's dead. My mom said so," she said.

"He is not dead!" I screamed at her. "Mom said he would be home later, that he was in a car accident, but not really hurt bad. You're lying!"

I ran, crying, into the kitchen, where Gram was standing with Mom, Aunt Sandy, and my other aunt, Helen.

"Kelly is being mean!" I shouted. "She told me Ritchie is dead. She's lying!"

The look on their faces scared me.

"It's not true, is it?" I wailed. "He isn't dead, is he?" And then directly to my mother, "You said he was okay and would be home tonight."

Without answering, she waved me back into the living room. As I ran back, my thoughts swirled around like a tornado. Aunt Helen followed and sat beside me.

"Everything's going to be okay. It's all going to be all right," she said over and over as she put her arm around me.

I fell asleep crying and woke up later that afternoon. Everyone was gone except for Gram. She was in the kitchen making dinner, and it smelled good. I hadn't eaten anything all day. Everything seemed normal, and I didn't say anything about Ritchie. I thought it must have been a bad dream, and I dared not say anything because I didn't want it to be true.

When dinner was ready, Gram and I sat at the table eating, my mind still going over the bad dream.

"You'll sleep here tonight," she said.

"Is she bringing Ritchie home from the hospital tonight?" I asked. "Because I want to be home to see him."

She stopped eating and said to me in a very soft voice, "He isn't coming home. He is gone. I am sorry, honey."

The next few days were a blur. Lots of visitors, people I didn't know, came over with pans of food. My mother never talked to me during this time. Not a word. She was either not there or upstairs, and I was not allowed to see her because she wanted to be alone.

The following Monday, however, she woke me up. "Get dressed," she said. "You're going to school."

Startled, I jumped out of bed and got dressed. As we drove, I watched the houses that we passed, wishing we were going to Gram's instead of school. She dropped me off in front of the main entrance. She didn't speak or even turn her head to tell me to get out, and as soon as I shut the car door, she drove off. As I walked toward the big metal double doors, I was met by my first-grade teacher and another lady who worked in the school office.

"I'm so sorry about your dad," my teacher said as we walked down the empty hall toward my classroom. We were late, and class had already started. I heard my teacher and the office lady whispering to each other behind me. "I can't believe they sent her back so early," said my teacher.

"I know. It's too soon," said the office lady. Only I didn't realize they were talking about me. Everything around me seemed like it was happening to someone else. Like I wasn't quite there. I couldn't absorb the school, the teacher, or the kids around me. They were busy in their world, and I was swimming in slow motion, just trying to keep moving forward.

When class started, my teacher, Mrs. Whitaker, a very pretty young woman, tall and slim with her hair pulled into a bun on top of her head, stood in front of the class and announced, "Good morning, class. Kim's family has suffered a loss. I need you all to be kind to her because losing a loved one is really hard."

Her words swirled through my head like the wind when the car windows are open. I started to feel hot and sick to my stomach as the kids stared at me. Some whispered to one another. Others just stared at me like they expected me to tell them what happened. Like I should explain to them why they had to be kind to me. My head started to spin, and I could hear my heart pounding in my chest, the whispers and staring finally overtaking me, and I blurted out, "My stepdad died in a car accident."

I thought that would make them stop staring, but it didn't. They whispered more, and the room got hotter. Mrs. Whitaker walked toward me. Her face looked all twisted, and her eyes sad. She stared at me, holding her hand out as she got close. By then, I was crying uncontrollably, and I felt so scared and alone. When she reached my desk, she rubbed my back. As I sat there sobbing, the chunky boy with curly brown hair and glasses who sat in front of me said very matter-of-factly, "He wasn't killed in a car accident. My parents said he was stabbed by a bunch of people, and that's how he died."

With that, the room started to spin, and everything went black.

Chapter 5

I don't think Gram and my aunts wondered whether my mom told me the truth about how Ritchie died. His death was never really brought up around me. There was lots of quiet talk among them, and it always stopped as soon as I came close.

"Mom, did Ritchie really die in a car accident?" I asked one day. "Because kids at school said he was stabbed by a bunch of people."

She twisted her face to look like someone had just asked her to eat something disgusting. Like my question — and me — were smelly socks shoved in her face. She turned to me with stone-cold eyes and hissed, "For the last time, he died in a car accident. Stop crying. For God's sake, it's not like he was your real dad anyway."

I wish she had just taken the belt to me. The sting of the leather strap and the welt it would have left would slowly fade. Those words, *real dad,* never did. Even though I called him Ritchie, I always thought of him as my dad. At six years old, I was told the man I had loved and thought of as my dad wasn't real. I didn't understand why she would say this. He was very real, and now he was gone. The hole he left in my life was great, and no one would talk to me about him. It was like he had never existed in the first place.

As hard as losing him was, the worst was yet to come.

School became unbearable. I had already been the odd kid, the one who'd had a dead moose hanging from a tree for everyone on bus #19 to see on the first day of kindergarten. The one who wore homemade, mismatched, and often dirty clothes to school because that was all she had. The one whose stepfather's murder was all over the news and on the front page of the newspaper. The one who came to school and fainted in front of the entire class when the truth was blurted out to her. It was the topic at the dinner table in many people's homes. Within a few days, the entire school knew.

Kids and adults stared at me. I could hear their whispers, and kids picked on me on the bus. I would start crying, which only made things worse. A girl named Brenda mocked me on the bus. "What's the matter, baby? Isn't your daddy coming to save you?" she'd taunt. "No, he isn't because he's dead!" And then she'd laugh. She would push me as I got off the bus and call me names almost every day.

Other girls picked on me, too. They'd push me to the ground, pull my hair, and trip me as I walked to my seat on the bus. After they got me to the ground, they'd laugh at me sitting there, crying and hoping someone would come over and help, but no one ever did. "Look at the baby!" They would taunt. I had no idea how to make it stop.

It got so bad that I started going to the school nurse complaining of being sick almost every day just so I wouldn't have to ride the bus home. The nurse would call Gram or Mom to come pick me up. Sometimes Mom would come, but most of the time, she wouldn't, and Gram came instead. When Mom did come, she would make me go to my room and not come out, like when I was four. Usually, I would lie on the floor and trace the cheerful flower print on my linoleum floor with my finger. Following the dark lines against the bright flowers over and over soothed me and took my mind off whatever was happening. Sometimes I did this for hours.

The name-calling continued throughout first grade, but being pushed and tripped and having my hair pulled stopped for the most part, thanks to the bus driver, who moved me to the front of the bus. I figured she moved me because I cried a lot and didn't have friends, and she wanted to keep an eye on me. It never occurred to me that she was trying to protect me — I was hit and pushed at home, too, and no one protected me there — but I was grateful nonetheless. Kids continued to make fun of me and give me dirty looks as they passed by, but at least I had one safe place... until I got home, anyway.

Chapter 6

Mom always slept all day. I got myself up for school and dressed myself in the cleanest clothes I could find from the piles on the floor. If she did do laundry, the clothes would sit in the washer for days, growing stinky and black from mildew. The clothes I wore more than once smelled like pee because I was afraid to bring attention to myself during class, and I ended up peeing a little in my pants every day.

Most days, when I came home from school, I opened the front door to a darkened room, except for the glow from the black-and-white TV and the end of Mom's cigarette as she lay passed out in the pullout sofa from the night before. David, now age two, was either still in his pajamas, his diaper full and hanging off him like a wet sack of potatoes, or running around naked.

I always had chores ahead of me. I cleaned the house, took care of my brother, and tried to figure out what the two of us should eat for dinner. Infrequently, she would make dinner — usually, something from a can like peas or Chef Boyardee ravioli. Peas were my favorite, even cold. Every once in a while, she would make something that required more than a saucepan. On these rare occasions, she attempted to clean up after herself, throwing filthy pans in the sink to soak. These pans soaked for days and always made the house smell like rotting garbage.

One day, I came home from school and was hit with a horrible odor when I opened the door. Mom was in the bathroom. I knew this because the bathroom door was cracked open and a trail of gray cigarette smoke drifted into the hall outside it. In addition to the typical stench of her body odor, cigarette smoke, and trash, I smelled a different pungent odor. I followed the smell, through the dark, to the tiny, dilapidated kitchen at the back of the house. The sink was full of dirty dishes, one of which was a pan from days earlier that had been soaking. I stepped on my tiptoes to look inside. It was full of stagnant water and had food crusted on the edges.

I looked closer and saw tiny white worms crawling around in the pan. Maggots. Tons of them. The smell was so bad I almost vomited.

"You need to clean this pan right now," Mom snapped from behind me.

Horrified, I pointed up at the maggots. "I don't want to touch them."

She laughed. "Get it done. And it better be spotless, along with the rest of the dishes."

She went outside, sat down on the porch, and lit a cigarette. This was her daily afternoon ritual. Sleep until I got home, my brother penned up in his crib with multiple bottles, some empty, some curdled, in a sopping-wet diaper. Then, when I came home, she'd get him out of the crib, change his diaper, and take him outside with her. Today wasn't any different.

Once she had shut the door, I looked again at the pan, knowing there was no way I was going to put my hand anywhere near the slimy food and little worms. So I opened a grocery bag, picked up the pan with paper towels, and shoved it in the bag. The smell was so bad, that I threw up in my mouth a little. I took the bag out the back door and threw it in the trash can. Somehow, it didn't occur to me that this wasn't a foolproof plan.

A couple of minutes later, she yelled for me to come outside. My heart sank. I was in big trouble.

"Did you clean the pan?" she asked.

"Yes," I lied, my heart beating so hard and fast that I could hear the beats in my ears.

"Where is it?" she demanded.

I paused for a minute, not knowing what to do or say. I knew the truth would bring on the wrath of the belt. So, I tried another lie. By now, I was crying — not fake tears to get away with a lie, but tears of fear of what would happen to me if that lie didn't work.

"I'm sorry, Mommy," I said. "It's not clean. I tried my best, but it was uncleanable. The food was too stuck on."

Instantly, she grabbed my arm and walked me to the side of the house where the trash can was. I knew I was getting the belt.

"I'm sorry, Mommy! I'm sorry, Mommy!" I repeated.

She lifted the trash can lid, pulled out the paper bag with the maggot-ridden pan, and took her cigarette out of her mouth. She shoved the pan at me, but I didn't take it, afraid to touch what was crawling around the edges, and the pan fell to the ground.

"Pick it up!" she yelled.

I was frozen with fear, sobbing, "Please don't make me touch it. Please, Mommy, *please!!!* I'm scared of the worms. Please, Mommy!"

Then she grabbed my hand, pulling me toward the monstrosity, and I pulled away. She was furious. She grabbed the hair on top of my head and pushed me down toward the pan. I screamed in pain and fear.

"Pick up the pan, Kim," she repeated. "Pick up the goddamn pan!"

Still sobbing, but harder now and begging her in between sobs for her not to hit me, she let go of my hair, grabbed my arm, took the cigarette from the corner of her mouth, and pressed the red-hot end into my forearm. The pain was so intense, I could hardly breathe. I had no idea what she would do next, and not knowing was almost as terrifying as whatever she would actually do.

"Pick up the goddamn pan!" she yelled again.

My arm was throbbing. I could see the perfect circle where the cigarette had been burned into it. I was crying so hard I couldn't catch my breath, which only made her angrier. Terrified that she would burn me again, I somehow managed to pick up the pan with my other hand.

She grabbed my burned arm and squeezed it hard right where the burn was. Searing pain radiated through my body.

"Get your ass in that kitchen and make this goddamn pan spotless!" she yelled, and dragged me inside.

This was the first of many burns Mom gave me. Most of the burns were done in rage, but some were done for no reason, as though she enjoyed it and just wanted a laugh when I cried out in shock and pain. The scars on my legs, arms, and hands have faded over time. Usually, I could hide them by wearing pants and long-sleeved shirts.

The night before our school pictures, I had taken out the trash and forgot to put the lid on the can. That next morning, the trash was all over the yard, and she was fuming.

"Get your ass outside and pick up every goddamn piece of trash," she yelled.

I had gotten up early to figure out what to wear for pictures. My closet didn't have much, and the rest of my clothes were dirty. I decided on the pink-and-white seersucker top Gram had made. When she yelled this to me, I was standing in front of the mirror, admiring how I looked. She found me in the bathroom and again yelled at me to go pick up the trash.

"But I will be dirty for my pictures," I said.

Without hesitation, she reached over and pushed her cigarette into my neck, right in front. I screamed and winced in pain.

"Clean it up," she said, as she turned around and left me standing in the bathroom.

I never told my aunts or grandmother about the burns. I was afraid Mom would find out — and of what she would do to me when she did. But I was also embarrassed. In some way, I thought maybe I deserved them. I didn't want my family to know I was a child who deserved such a punishment.

At night, I lay awake, dreading school the next day. After she thought we were asleep, I'd hear the front door open and shut. After a few moments, her engine whined as she tried to start her car, and then the low roar once she did. And she was gone. If David woke up, I got him milk for his bottle. I wasn't quite big enough to lift him out of his crib, but I could reach the milk and pour it, even if the gallon jug was full. I was six, and even though I was tall for my age, I still struggled trying to handle a milk jug without spilling it. Often, I would use whatever clothing I was wearing to sop up the spill so that I wouldn't be in trouble when she got home. Even though the house was full of trash, with clothes piled everywhere, ashtrays full of ash and cigarette butts, and the kitchen sink full of dishes, I knew if I spilled, she would punish me. I really didn't know what I was doing, but I knew I had to be the parent and that David needed me. Then I would crawl back into bed, terrified, sometimes for what seemed like hours, until I heard the car pull into the driveway. I never said anything to anyone for fear of being spanked and punished, and worse, that if I did, maybe she would never come back.

Chapter 7

When I was almost seven, I moved back in with Gram. This meant I got to go to a different school — one where kids didn't know me as the kid whose dad got murdered or who wore dirty clothes and cried a lot. And more important, my mother and brother didn't move with me. I didn't know why, and I didn't know where they were, and I didn't care. I was safe and happy. It was the beginning of summer. Kids played outside, the ice cream man came every afternoon, and my cousins visited us sometimes. The dark shadows of my mother disappeared.

I had my own room upstairs, and although I slept with Gram most nights, this room of mine was so pretty. The ceiling in the front of the room sloped down because it was an old, brick, colonial house that my grandfather built years before I was born. It had dark-red brick with white shutters. The front window let warm rays of sunlight flood into the room.

I felt safe at Gram's. During the daytime, her room was always clean and bright, and on her nightstand, she had a small, green Baby Ben alarm clock that she had to wind every night before we turned off the bedside lamp. She always made her bed in the mornings and taught me how to do hospital corners, so the bed looked properly made.

After saying the Lord's Prayer, she often told me stories of when I was a baby. About how I slept in the bottom drawer of her dresser, how my infant sleeping gowns became nightshirts as I grew. How hurt and sad she and my grandfather were when my mother took me away as a baby and how happy they were when I came back a few months later. As she tucked me in, she always said, "I love you. Sweet dreams."

I loved sitting in the living room, the fireplace aglow with a warmth that soaked into your skin, much like the rays of the sun on a warm

August day. Gram would sit in her chair crocheting an afghan, watching an old movie on TV. I would lie on the teal-green carpet next to the old octagon table that kept her yarn and hooks hidden inside. Somewhere in this cabinet was always a bag of candy, usually Reese's Peanut Butter Cups, or a full-size Hershey bar. She'd reach in and pull out the hidden treat, saying, "Oh, look what I found! Guess we should have just a little bit, so there is more for tomorrow."

I would get one flat, round Reese's cup or one rectangular Hershey square from the bar. Delectable. And, of course, I'd search for it the next day when she wasn't looking and finish it off. She never seemed to mind.

My uncle Bobby also lived in the house with us. He looked different. He had a grown man's body, but he acted like a child. Gram said he had mongolism. I had no clue what that was. He had small eyes and a drawn, child-like face. He would make Gram mad because he wouldn't help with chores. If she yelled at him, he would yell back and either go ride his bike or shut himself in his room. Gram didn't seem to understand him. Maybe she was afraid because she blamed herself for him being born that way.

Gram had a hard life growing up. She told me stories as we worked in the garden. Raised during the depression, she valued every dollar like it was her last. She sewed clothes to save money, made soap from lard, and grew fresh vegetables, so we always had food to eat. She worked hard to maintain her home. After she had raised Uncle Bobby, she got stuck raising me. Her husband, Grandpa Robert, had died almost four years earlier, when she was 58 and Uncle Bobby was in his mid-twenties. But even on a fixed income, she made it work. I was oblivious to her financial struggles, though. I just loved her attention, spending time with her, and our special quiet talks after we said the Lord's Prayer.

She'd often send me out to pick blackberries — a chore I was not fond of. The other kids would be outside playing kickball, and I could hear them laughing and having fun. Wanting so much to play, I'd toss four of the eight one-pint baskets over the bank at the dead end and then mysteriously return with only four as if that were all she gave me. I thought I was getting away with it, too.

"All done!" I said, champing at the bit for my turn to kick the red, firm kickball.

"Are these all of the baskets I gave you?"

"Yes," I lied. "Now can I go play...please?"

"Go play, but be in at dark," she relented.

And off I went.

She must have known, but she never called me out on my lies.

With Gram, I didn't worry that a little fib would result in a beating or getting burned by a cigarette. She never said things like, "If you don't stop crying, I will duct tape your mouth shut and put you in a home for unwanted kids." That was Mom's go-to when I was crying from her beating me. It only made me cry harder, though. I also didn't worry about disappointing Gram. One time with Mom, I didn't climb all the way up on the monkey bars because I was terrified that if I fell, no one would help me. At times like that, or if I spoke back to her or didn't take care of my brother the way she thought I should, she'd say, "I should have taken a coat hanger and gotten rid of you when I found out I was pregnant." I didn't understand what a coat hanger had to do with me, but I got the gist. Gram didn't talk about coat hangers, homes for unwanted kids, or getting rid of me. She just let me be myself.

Everything was going great at Gram's that summer... until Mom and David moved in. I felt like they were strangers, not belonging to our little family. Gram would ask for her to help around the house, and Mom would call her an "old battle-ax" and tell her not to boss her around. They fought a lot, mostly because Mom never picked up after herself. She and David were hardly home during the day, and they missed dinner most nights, which didn't bother me at all.

One day my mother had to go somewhere, and she left David and me with Gram. It wasn't unusual for her to leave me with Gram, but she rarely left my brother with us. About an hour after she left, we were outside playing, and he got mad at me because I wouldn't give him my ball. He picked up a stick and struck my head, scratching my face and making a deep cut just under my eye. Even at three years old, he was extremely strong and had the same hateful spirit my mother did toward me. I was crying loudly and running away from him because he still had the stick and was chasing me with it toward the house.

Gram must have heard the commotion because she burst out the front door to see what was happening. As soon as I saw her, I made a beeline to where she stood, David just a few steps behind. She saw my face with the small trickle of blood running down my cheek and my brother running at me with the stick. With one big swoop, she grabbed my brother by the arm and the stick with her other hand. He was now screaming and trying to bite and kick her. She plopped this raging three-year-old on the ground, took the stick, and swatted him on the behind with it. In all the commotion, we didn't notice Mom had come home. She had been walking toward the house as Gram swatted my brother.

"Don't you lay one more finger on him!" she screamed.

We all froze, except for David, who started to wail like he was dying and ran to her. She scooped him up, walked up to Gram with her eyes glaring, and poked Gram hard in the chest. "Don't you ever lay another fucking finger on my son, ever. You will have to deal with me if you do."

She stomped past me. My brother tried to kick me in the head as he was carried into the house, a big smile on his face. Gram didn't say a word after my mother went inside, and neither did I. But at that moment, I knew that she was as afraid of my mother as I was and that it was better to be quiet.

A couple weeks later, Mom came home and announced, "We are going to California to visit Aunt Thelma." I thought she was referring to her and David, so I shrugged it off and went into the kitchen. Following behind me, she said, "Aren't you excited, Kim? You get to go on a plane!"

My ears were pretty sure they heard her wrong. *She's not taking me*, I thought. *She never takes me anywhere.* I didn't reply, and she repeated herself — a bit angrily this time. I quickly shook my head, still trying to figure out why I got to go with her. *Maybe*, I thought, *she wanted it to be just her and me to make up for all the bad things she had done and said to me.* Then I was excited. *I get to go on a plane to California, just me and Mom. And she wanted me to go. Just me.*

In my excitement, I asked, "Will David stay with Gram while we are gone?" Her response was fast and cut deep. "No, he is coming. Don't be stupid. I would never leave him behind."

Of course, I thought and sulked off to my room. The next day, Gram asked Mom why she wanted to go to California with two small kids by herself. It would be expensive for Mom and a burden on Aunt Thelma, Gram's sister, to take care of visitors. She still worked full-time as a hairdresser in Santa Monica. Mom ignored her, and before I knew it, we were on a plane.

Chapter 8

I got motion-sick, so as soon as we took off, I closed my eyes and made myself fall asleep. The last thing I wanted was to vomit in the Wonder Bread plastic bag Gram had given to me before we left. "Just in case," she had said as she handed me the crumpled plastic bag. Thank God I slept through the entire flight, waking as we bumped down onto the runway. I had never met my great aunt, so I didn't know what to expect. I was very nervous. She picked us up at the curb at the airport in a big, light-blue Oldsmobile with a white top. It was the prettiest car I had ever seen! She jumped out of the car when she saw us walking toward this blue beauty and greeted us with a slight southern drawl and hugs.

She had bright blonde hair, curled, with every piece in place. She wore red lipstick, a bright scarf tied around her neck, and a pretty pink dress. In my mind, all I could think of was that she was so pretty and smelled so nice — like the roses that grew in Gram's yard. She was also very warm and welcoming, asking me about my favorite subject in school, who my friends were back home, and, once we were in the car heading to her house, if I liked to dance and listen to music. Even though I was sitting in the backseat, she would look in the rearview mirror as we chatted, smiling and making eye contact as much as she could. At stop lights, she would even turn her head so that she could see me as we talked. She was Gram's sister but had the exact opposite personality. Gram was always worried, tired, and sad. She hardly smiled and didn't wear anything bright or fashionable, and we didn't have many conversations at all. Her sister was happy and had a smile that lit up her face. I liked her instantly.

She spoke to my mother as we drove, saying how sorry she was about my stepdad dying and how hard it must be raising two small children all by herself. As usual, my mother milked it, saying she had to work two jobs just to keep up and that often that still wasn't enough. I was used to her doing this, making people feel bad for her, so they would give her money. She did this to Gram's brother and sister-in-law all the time. My mother didn't have two jobs. She didn't even have one most of the time. She received Social Security and veterans benefit checks every month and was lazy, so she lived off of them instead of working. I always felt uncomfortable when she played on people's emotions, and embarrassed, too. I didn't understand why she didn't even try to work but would rather take money from people who pitied her.

By the time we arrived at Aunt Thelma's house, I was starting to feel nauseated from the ride and thankful to be out of a moving vehicle finally. Her home was a single-story ranch with orange trees in the front yard. The inside was clean and bright and smelled like cake. She had baked a buttermilk pound cake before she came to pick us up, and the sweet smell welcomed us as soon as we walked in the door.

I went and played with her dog on the sun porch while she and Mom had coffee and talked in the kitchen with David. I remember hearing Aunt Thelma say how surprised she was when my mother called and told her we'd be visiting. "Do you have any other plans while you're here?" she asked Mom. The sun porch was connected to the back of the kitchen. I could hear their conversation but didn't really pay attention. Instead, I brushed the fluffy cockapoo that came over and sat on my lap, soaking up the attention. But when she asked about "other plans," my ears perked up. What were our other plans? I wanted to go to Disneyland and knew it was close by because of the billboards I saw on the drive from the airport. I loved Mickey and Minnie Mouse, and going to Disneyland where they lived would be a dream come true! Disneyland was not in her plans, but going to visit her uncle was. I had no idea who this uncle was, except that he was one of Gram's younger brothers, and he also lived in California. My mother asked so many questions about this uncle. Is he married? Does his son still live with him? And on and on. I lost interest in the conversation and went back to playing with the dog, dreams of Disney still in my head.

As we were getting ready for bed, I asked Mom, "Could we go to Disneyland to see Mickey and Minnie?"

"It costs too much money. Be grateful that I brought you here, and go to bed."

The next day, I woke up to my mother barking orders at me.

"Get dressed. We're leaving."

She had found a daycare in the yellow pages that would take David for the day, so we borrowed Aunt Thelma's car and left, all the while hoping, *imagining*, that she had changed her mind and we were going to Disneyland. But I didn't say a word because I didn't want to say something that would make her mad and change her mind. After we dropped my brother off, we got on a big highway and drove for what seemed to be a long time, going farther and farther from the city. Finally, we exited the highway and drove until we reached a big open area full of dirt, where motorized dirt bikes were zipping around. *This isn't Disneyland,* I thought to myself as my heart sank. By this time, I had used the Wonder Bread bag twice and felt like I needed to vomit again. She drove past the large dirt lot and stopped at an old, silver trailer with an old truck in front of it. The trailer was nestled around tall trees and had a lawn chair next to the wood steps that sat on the side of the trailer and led to the front door. She got out of the car and told me to get out as well. I stunk like vomit, and the bag, half full, was still clenched in my hand. And I had to pee really bad.

She took the lawn chair, moved it to the side of the trailer, and ordered me to sit there and not move. "I won't be long," she said.

"I have to go to the bathroom. Can I please go inside?"

"If you get out of this chair, I will beat your ass." She didn't even address the having-to-pee issue. So, there I sat, still holding the plastic bag half full of vomit, with a wet spot on my pants, where I peed a little trying to hold it in, in the middle of nowhere, in front of an old trailer that my mother disappeared into.

After about ten minutes, I gave up trying to hold in the pee and set the vomit bag on the ground beside me. There I sat in my wet pants for what seemed like hours. When she finally came out, she grabbed my arm and pulled me toward the car. I never saw who lived in that trailer, only a shadow of a man at the door as we drove off.

"Who is that man?" I asked as we drove off. "Why did we come here?"

She didn't answer my questions that day, and it would be decades before I learned the truth.

My pants were dry by now, and I was hungry but too afraid to say anything because she was already upset. Her curses filled the car on the way back to Aunt Thelma's house. She was so mad that she hit the dash of the car with her fist. By the time we got back to pick up my brother, she had calmed down. He came out of daycare with a piece of construction paper with scribbles all over it. I was so jealous that he got to have fun, and I had to sit and do nothing. By the time we got to the house, I was mad, hungry, and worried that I stank so bad Aunt Thelma would notice. Thankfully, I was able to run inside without seeing anyone and change my clothes.

When I came out, Aunt Thelma was in the kitchen making dinner. She had made meatloaf and potatoes, which looked and smelled amazing to me and my empty stomach.

"Kim, what fun things did you and your mom do today?" she asked after we sat down to eat.

I nearly choked on the food in my mouth. I guess my mother told her we were going to be doing something fun when she asked to borrow her car. I wanted to set the story straight. The anger inside me was boiling up. I wanted to tell her about how my day completely sucked. I was ready to tell her exactly how fun it was to take a long car ride that made me vomit. That I sat in a chair outside for hours, that I peed my pants because I couldn't get up for fear of being beaten. I wanted to tell her exactly what kind of day it was. I knew Mom wouldn't take the belt to me here because she didn't want anyone to hear me crying and begging her to stop. As I worked up my nerve, I felt my mother's hand on my leg under the table. She pinched my thigh — hard. I looked at her and saw her blue eyes piercing through me, warning me not to say a goddamn word — or else. And I knew what "or else" meant.

Tears ran down my face.

"I had a fun day, thank you." I lied.

Aunt Thelma looked at me with concern. "Well, if you had fun, then why are you crying?"

Without thinking, I blurted out, "Because I thought we were going to Disneyland to see Minnie and Mickey, but we didn't."

I was sobbing. Exhausted from the horrible day, scared of my mother's wrath, and embarrassed for being such a baby in front of my great aunt, I was more than surprised when she reached across the table and took my hand to console me. It was something very unfamiliar to me, and I immediately pulled my hand away and stopped crying. Kindness, understanding, and a kind human touch were things I craved but didn't know how to receive. My Gram loved me, this I knew, and I knew I was safe with her. But this was different. I hardly knew this sweet person, and she was so nice to me and loving. I didn't understand why.

Even though I pulled away, she continued to speak in a soft tone. She said in her southern drawl, "Well then, tomorrow you and your mother will go to Disneyland. My treat! And make sure you tell Mickey and Minnie 'hi' for me."

What?!? Had I heard her correctly? Disneyland??? I was ecstatic and ran around the table and gave her a hug, no hesitation. Joy and happiness had overcome my fear of being hugged.

"Oh, Aunt Thelma, thank you for the kind offer, but I don't think I can possibly handle both of them on my own all day at Disneyland. David's too little." Mom protested.

"It's no problem at all. I'm home tomorrow, and he can stay here with me." Aunt Thelma assured her. "It will be a good idea for just the two of you to spend a fun day together."

My mother looked over at me with the well-known glare that only I noticed. "Get your butt up, put your pajamas on, and go to bed." She told me. I scrambled up and did just what she said without a peep. I wasn't going to let anything get in the way of seeing Mickey and Minnie!

Chapter 9

The excitement I felt as we pulled into the park was palpable. There were so many cars parked in the lot and so many families walking toward the gate. I could hear music playing from a distance, happy music from what sounded like a brass jazz band. As we walked toward the gate, I saw a red balloon floating up toward the sky. It was in the shape of Mickey's head, dancing in the sky to the beat of the music, floating upward toward the sun in slow motion, almost like the balloon was trying to go back to the child who forgot to hold on tight to the white cotton string.

"We are only staying for a couple hours. And if you ask for anything, we're leaving," she said as we got out of the car.

I barely heard her. I was too busy thinking about meeting Mickey and Minnie, and even Donald, although he wasn't my favorite character. He was always angry and yelling about or at someone. I had my share of that at home. But Mickey and Minnie always smiled and seemed so friendly, and on that day, I was going to get to meet them. *Maybe they will even give me a hug like they did to the kids they met on their TV show!* The thought was almost too much to contain.

My heart was skipping beats as I walked quickly to the line to enter the park. My mother lagged behind, constantly pulling the back of my shirt toward her. She was not happy to be here, having been guilted into it by my emotional breakdown the night before.

Once we got through the line to buy the tickets and then another long line to enter the park, my eyes couldn't believe what they were seeing. Brightly painted buildings on either side of the street, a person holding a whole bunch of the Mickey balloons, kids surrounding this person pointing at the one they wanted, and parents handing money over as each balloon was handed out to a child. I stopped myself from asking if I, too, could have one. I *really* wanted one, but I wanted to see Mickey and Minnie more. So I didn't say a peep as we walked down this magical street, without a balloon. Neither of us said a word, both having our own reasons.

At the end of the main street was something I had only seen on TV. Cinderella's castle, right in front of my eyes. I looked up toward the highest part of the castle, the sun not allowing me to see much except the outline of the castle with bright spots blocking my vision. I tried to see if Tinkerbell was perched on top, waiting to fly down and sprinkle Pixie dust as she did on TV, but the sun shined too brightly. I wondered if it was protecting the place where Tinkerbell would hide until she was safe from Captain Hook and the gator. Yes, I decided, that must be it, smiling to myself for being so smart to figure this out all by myself.

Once we walked through the middle of the castle, disappointed that we couldn't look through all the rooms, we stood in front of a bunch of amusement rides. Still no Mickey or Minnie. A carousel ride had brightly painted horses spinning around in a circle going up and down as if they were running up and down small hills trying to pass the horse in front of them but were never able to. There was another ride with about 12 Dumbo elephants with children and parents sitting in them holding a metal bar. The flying elephants were spinning in a similar circle. Some were flying way up high, others low, and some would bounce from high to low and back to high again. Just watching both of these rides made me dizzy and sick to my stomach. I was actually happy that we didn't come to ride rides. Not only did I get motion sick, but I was also terribly afraid of heights. My mother knew this very well and would try to make me overcome this fear by forcing me to climb to the top of the jungle gym at the park while I cried and begged to do anything else.

"If you don't go to the top, I'll beat your ass and make you wish you had," she would threaten.

I wanted to be brave enough to reach the top, like all the normal kids did, and I hated myself because I was too afraid. I thought, *What if I fall? No one will catch me. No one will be there to help me if I get hurt, especially not my mother.* This I was sure of, even at the tender age of seven. So instead, I chose being called "fat," "stupid," and "coward." And I got the beating I was promised because I failed to reach the top, every time. The insults and injuries I was familiar with and knew that although they stung, I could make it through a belt across the back of my legs, a cigarette being pushed into my arm, and being called a wimp and retarded. None of those were as bad as being at the top of the monkey bars.

How I didn't know that Disneyland was mostly scary rides is beyond me. In my mind, Disneyland was full of all the Disney characters, a place people went to meet them and see magic. It was where Tinkerbell spread Pixie dust, Peter Pan fought Captain Hook, Cinderella danced with Prince Charming, Snow White sang with the seven dwarfs, and Mickey and Minnie held hands as they greeted everyone, giggling in joy and hugging everyone they met.

My mother must have seen the expression on my face because she said, "Get in line for the Dumbo ride, Kim. Hurry up! It's about to start."

"I don't want to," I said immediately. "I'm scared."

At this, she grabbed my arm and dragged me to the end of the line.

"This is what you wanted. Disneyland — bitching and complaining to anyone who would listen," she snarked. "Well, hear me when I say you are going to ride every goddamn ride in this park!"

She made me ride Dumbo, crying and terrified until I realized if I didn't touch the bar in front of me, I stayed low to the ground and just went in circles. *Not too bad,* I thought. And that is what I did, just sat there at ground level, going in circles. Seeing her pissed-off face, yelling at me on every rotation to pull the bar.

I never did.

And she was mad. She grabbed my arm as soon as I got off the ride and squeezed it hard.

"That's a baby ride," she said.

She dragged me across the park. We passed a donkey ride with real donkeys, hoping we were stopping at this ride. I loved horses and donkeys as a child, but no such luck. We came to a sign that said something about a flight to the moon but saw no ride. As we got in line, I noticed how dark it was, thinking maybe this ride was like the planetarium I went to for a class field trip I had gone to earlier that year. We sat in a big, dark room with a domed roof, where stars, comets, and the Milky Way shined above brightly. As we got closer to the front of the line, I could hear screeching from people, the sound of something coming to a fast halt, and then metal-on-metal sounds like a rocket taking off, except this rocket was on a metal track.

This sound was confirmed as we reached the front of the line. I saw white-painted metal pods that looked like something from NASA linked together in the darkness. People got off, and the empty pods rolled to the front of the line where I stood, my mother still gripping my arm so hard that it throbbed. Now the only thing I felt was fear of having to get into that white pod. We were at the beginning of the line, which meant we had to get into the front pod. Once the pod stopped, she dragged me and gave the ticket person one ticket.

"Are you riding?" the nervous young attendant asked.

"No," she replied. "She'll be riding alone."

She couldn't be serious.

"Get in," she said.

"Nooooo! Please, please, please!" I begged.

Mom pulled me over to the pod and shoved me into it, glaring at me as I begged not to ride. The young attendant stood there watching. The look on her face showed she didn't exactly know what to do. I could tell my mom was too much for her, too.

The attendant addressed Mom quietly, not sure what to say. I was crying, and Mom was growling at me to get on the ride.

"She can get off," the attendant said nervously. "I'll give you your ticket back. It's no problem."

Mom looked at the ride attendant with the same piercing look I knew only too well and said, "No. She's riding, and do not let her off."

Screaming, I saw the expression on the young attendant's face as she pushed the red button to start the ride. Our eyes met. She looked sorry... and scared. Even she was afraid of what would happen if she disobeyed my mother.

I closed my eyes and could feel the metal bar closing me in. I felt the pod start to move. Although my eyes were shut, I could see the bright neon lights through my eyelids. I felt the drops and jerks as I rounded corners, sobbing. I kept my eyes closed in terror the entire time. It felt like hours. Once it stopped, the imminent feeling of nausea came, and I threw up all over myself before I could get my balance to stand up and get off the ride.

I was still sobbing, and in between the sobs, puke ejected from my mouth. No one offered to help me. In fact, people were looking at me and laughing, including my mother, who had been waiting for me to arrive.

"You did it!" she said. "You didn't die, did you? Now stop crying and stop being a pussy."

I made myself calm down. I smelled like vomit, and I didn't want more people laughing at me because I was retarded and a baby. I looked at others that had ridden this ride. They were laughing and happy as they climbed out of their pods. I could hear her voice in my head, *chicken, weak, retarded.* I hated myself for not being brave and for being a disappointment and an embarrassment. *Why can't I be like everyone else?* I thought to myself. *If only I could be brave, maybe she would love me.* Because that is all I had ever wanted. Just to be good enough for her to accept me as she did my brother.

It was this line of thinking that got me into my next mess.

"Are you ready to ride another ride?" she asked.

"Yes," I said, trying to sound as brave and triumphant as possible. This was my chance to earn her love and respect and make her realize that I am brave and not retarded.

She chose The Haunted Mansion for my last ride. How befitting. My stepfather dead, murdered, and she wanted me to go into a haunted mansion with ghosts.

"I will ride with you," she said.

Although I was very afraid, I didn't beg to get out of line, and my anxiety decreased a bit, knowing I wasn't going to have to ride by myself. We entered the room "with no windows and no doors." I closed my eyes and put my fingers in my ears. I felt the room move like we were in a big elevator. When the moving stopped, I opened my eyes and saw all the people moving out through doors that appeared from nowhere. *Yes!!* I thought. *I did it!* I made it through The Haunted Mansion without being a display of vomit, weakness, or embarrassment. The crowd walked quickly over a bridge and through a dark room... but the exit was nowhere to be seen. Instead, ride buggies passed along on a conveyor belt, with people getting out and others getting in. A ride attendant asked the group in front of me, "How many?"

"Three," they replied.

"Car number 2," the attendant said.

Wait, what?!? "The ride isn't over?" I asked Mom.

"No, it hasn't started yet."

Fear came over me, and I made the mistake of becoming upset.

"I don't want to go on the ride," I told her.

"You're going," she said, grabbing my arm.

"How many in your group?" the attendant asked my mother.

"One," my mother stated flatly. "She will be riding alone."

WHAT?!?!

"I don't want to go. Please! I'm scared!" I cried, any courage I had mustered gone, and fear now in its place. The sobbing and pleading only made her more pissed. It always did. By this point, people were staring, and the attendant once again told my mother I didn't have to ride and that there was an exit we could take to get back into the park.

Mom glared at me and then at the attendant (again). Her voice was seething. "She IS going to ride this ride — mind your damn business."

She then leaned down and spoke softly in my ear while her grip tightened around my arm. "Get on the goddamn ride, Kim, so help me if you don't. I will pull down your pants in front of everyone and whip your ass till it bleeds."

She pointed me to the buggy at the front of the line. I remember climbing in the seat and hearing a spooky voice that came from nowhere, but was speaking to me directly, telling me to get inside. The metal bar moved close to me by itself. The voice then said something about ghosts and spirits coming to visit me.

The ride started. I was terrified. Ghosts and spirits were coming — from the dead — to see me. *What if they took me where my stepfather was? He was dead.* I closed my eyes and cried the entire ride. I was terrified that if I opened my eyes, the ghost would see me and make me a ghost, too. The ride seemed to last forever, and my eyes were sealed shut the entire time. I felt the doom buggy slow down and could tell we were no longer in a dark room, even with my eyes shut. I could see that the room had lightened up. I opened my eyes and saw myself in a mirror, and then all of a sudden, a ghost was sitting next to me. I moved as far over as I could in my seat and started to scream, shrill screams of horror that didn't stop until the ride came to an end. A person who worked at the ride came up to me to see if I was okay.

"The ghost is coming to get me and make me dead like my dad!" I repeated over and over.

She took me outside, where my mother was standing and smoking a cigarette. The nice worker who had tried to calm me and helped me find my mother started to explain.

"She was really scared on that ride. Really she shouldn't have —"

"Don't tell me what my kids should or shouldn't do. It's none of your business," My mother interrupted.

"Let's go, Kim. You ruined any chance you had to meet Mickey and Minnie. You are a crybaby, and Mickey and Minnie hate crybabies."

And with that, we left Disneyland.

"Did you two have a fun day?" Aunt Thelma asked as soon as we got in the door.

"Yes," I said. And then I went to the back room with my makeshift bed, which consisted of an air mattress on the floor, and buried my face in the pillow, so no one could hear my sobs as I tried to get the images out of my mind... spirits, ghosts, and her face when she said she wasn't going with me on the ride. The way the ride attendant looked at me as I begged to get off before she pushed the red Start button, and the motion sickness that I still felt. My heart hurt so much from what had happened that day. *What did I do wrong?* I wondered. The voice in my head kept replaying over and over, *You're stupid and a mistake. Everything you do is wrong. You should have been brave, not a crybaby. All of this is your fault. You should have never been born.* Just like she had told me so many times. I figured she had to be right.

I saw all the kids at Disneyland laughing and having fun. Not me. I ruined it for myself. Mickey and Minnie didn't want to meet me. How could they? I was an embarrassment and didn't appreciate the rides they had for kids to enjoy. I should have known that it was an amusement park, with rides. How stupid could I have been? If I hadn't cried, she would have ridden the ride like she said she was going to. *It's all your fault. You're not like normal kids.* The voice clamored in my head, and this was not the first time my mind reminded me that I just didn't fit in, and probably the thousandth time I had prayed that I could be normal, so she would love me. "I'm sorry, Mommy," I said out loud. "I will try to be better, so you don't wish I wasn't born. I promise."

We flew back home the next day. I kept quiet the entire ride to the airport, not wanting to upset Mom. I also didn't want Aunt Thelma to see all the bad things about me that my mother saw, so I pretended to sleep until we pulled up to the airport. Everyone got out of the car. Aunt Thelma opened the trunk and helped pull our suitcase out.

"You should visit more. It was so great to see you!" she said to my mother, who had my brother in one hand and her cigarette in the other. Aunt Thelma leaned down and gave me a hug. I just stood there, not hugging back. I wanted her to stop but also to never let go. She must have sensed my nervousness because she pulled back as she stood up.

"You're such a pretty little girl, Kimmy," she said. "You need to smile more!"

I couldn't believe my ears. *She thinks I'm pretty?!?* I wanted to be pretty, not awkward, chubby, and taller than all the other kids. I always had to wear pants that were two inches too short. A wave of warmth flushed my face, and I smiled so big that my eyes squinted shut. *She thinks I'm pretty.* I was in heaven until my mother scolded her for saying such things.

"Don't tell her that! It will go to her head!"

And from heaven I fell. The heaviness settled in again, Aunt Thelma's words snuffed out.

Why did my mother stop her? What did it mean to "go to my head?" I wondered. Who was that man in the door of the mobile home I sat in front of for hours a couple days ago? Why did we come here? These questions ran through my mind as I sat on the plane.

Chapter 10

For the next four and a half years, my mother and brother flopped at Gram's house on and off. I slept upstairs next to Gram's room, and they had the bedroom downstairs next to Uncle Bobby's room. Gram always yelled at them for not cleaning up after themselves when they stayed there. Mom lay in bed, eating at all hours of the night and smoking in the house. They came when she had no money and left when her checks came in, so she could pay bills at the shack we had lived in when Ritchie was alive.

I hated when they were there. During these years, she used the belt across my back and legs and reminded me that she should have used a coat hanger to get rid of me when she had the chance. She called me a slut, said I was fat, and told me she would send me to a girl's home. I could never figure out why she would beat and degrade me regularly. The only reason that came to mind was her saying, "Your mouth will be the death of you, Kim," her eyes glared as she swung the belt to the back of my legs. I'm not sure if she meant it, but she certainly could have killed me at any time without much more hate or effort than she was already exhibiting. I was grateful to have survived... to not have my head bashed in or be buried behind a house.

Because Gram was a Jehovah's Witness, we didn't celebrate regular holidays. She would cook a turkey in the fall with all the trimmings, but we didn't call it Thanksgiving. My aunts, their husbands, and my cousins would come over, and we would eat and play outside. Mom was nice to me when they visited, and I always begged for my cousins to spend the night. If they were over, I was safe. Or, I tried to get them to ask their parents if I could go to their house. Usually, the answer was no. They didn't like staying at Gram's, and I was known to be a conniver. I was plotting and planning to spend the night to escape, but my aunts and uncles just saw me as a child who wanted a sleepover and tried to manipulate my cousins into asking so maybe their parents would say yes. My efforts usually failed.

I wasn't allowed to celebrate Christmas, Halloween, Easter, or Valentine's Day. This also meant I couldn't participate in Christmas plays. I couldn't dress up for Halloween and show off my costume (not that I had one) as I went trick-or-treating down the hall, where teachers and staff passed out candy. I never got to pick out a special box of Valentine cards from Woolworths, carefully separating each one from the perforated sheets, being careful not to rip them, and assigning each card to the right person from the list of class members the teacher passed out before the school Valentine's Day party.

Gram firmly believed in her faith, which got her through many heartbreaks and hard times. She had many friends in her congregation, and to her, they were family. But to me, a child who already stuck out, this caused more negative attention. I had a fresh start when I moved into Gram's house. No one knew about my stepdad being murdered, and the name-calling and bullying had stopped.

So even though I had a new school and a new beginning, I stood out like a dirty feather in a sea of white ones. All the other kids got to join in the holiday fun. All the kids dressed up for Halloween and received carefully picked Valentines in the bright and cheery mailbox they had made from an old shoe box they brought from home. Everyone except me. I think I wanted to fit in more than celebrate a holiday. I wanted to not be left out. I wanted to be accepted and part of something fun.

In the fall of that year, I was eight. My great-aunt May and great-uncle Dick, Gram's brother and wife, came to visit. Whenever they came, they always brought a carton of Friendly's ice cream. As soon as Aunt May put her purse down, I excitedly ran to show her a picture of

Holly Hobbie, a stuffed doll from the Sears and Roebucks catalog. Aunt May was very fashionable and stylish, things I wanted to be, too, and I knew when I showed her Holly, she would see the beauty as I did. "Isn't she so pretty, Auntie May?" I asked as I showed her the torn catalog page. "I love her dress and prairie hat and her long braids and soft smile." I went on and on about this doll like she was the most valuable work of art ever. Aunt May listened carefully, smiling with a kind smile, bright with burgundy lipstick framing it perfectly.

"Maybe Santa will bring her for Christmas if you are a good girl," she said.

My heart sank. "Santa doesn't come here, Aunt May. I'm not supposed to believe in him." She continued to smile, but it was softer now. And out of respect for Gram and her religious beliefs just shook her head and said, "Well, let's eat some ice cream before it melts." And then she paused and said, "Always remember you should believe in things you don't see or understand. It's called faith. Faith gets us through all of the bad stuff."

After they left, I took the page from the catalog that had the one-inch tile photo of the Holly Hobbie that I wanted and placed it under my pillow. I wished for Santa to sneak her into my room. I promised Santa that I wouldn't tell anyone but would keep her safe and all to myself. I even made a deal with Santa, promising that I would take care of Holly, keep her clean, and love her every day if he would figure out a way to get her to me. I made this promise to Santa, God — anyone who was listening — every night after I said my prayers.

Right after Christmas, my mother took David and me to visit Uncle Dick and Aunt May. They had a beautiful home, so clean and cheery. It had three stories with shiny wood floors and a sweet boxer whose nails clicked as she walked through the room. She was old and almost blind. I would always sit and pet her, softly scratch behind her ears and the top of her head, speaking to her quietly. She would lie on the shiny floor and put her head in my lap, trusting what she couldn't see but could feel — and loving every minute of it.

After dinner that night, Aunt May called me from downstairs where the Christmas tree was. She asked me to grab the pair of scissors from the kitchen counter. I grabbed the black-handled metal Fiskars, which had a corner broken off at the tip of one of the blades, just like the pair Gram had on her sewing table. Making sure to hold them the way Gram had shown me, blades pointed down, I walked down the small flight of stairs and saw my auntie sitting on the floor in front of the softly lit Christmas tree, all the presents now gone and in the hands of the lucky person for whom they had been intended. As I walked toward my aunt, wondering what in the world she needed scissors for, she asked me to sit beside her for a second and close my eyes. I handed her the scissors as I sat down, wondering why but not saying a word. I heard footsteps and paper rustling. Finally, she said, "Okay, open your eyes."

I opened my eyes, and before me were two beautifully wrapped presents, both wrapped in red paper with white bows. One large and one small. My heart began to race. *Could she be here? Did Santa hear my prayers? Please, please, let Holly be in one of these boxes.*

Aunt May handed me back the scissors and said, "Go ahead. They are BOTH for you. Santa dropped them off because he knew you would be coming over for dinner tonight. He knows everything you know."

Sizing up both of the boxes, I chose the smaller one first. I cut the ribbon with the scissors and ripped the wrapping paper off at lightning speed. The top of the box had been Scotch-taped to the bottom and was a challenge to take apart. But I got through it, and through the tissue paper, I could see white, quilted clothing. As I pulled the tissue paper out, I noticed that the clothing was actually a robe. It was white with small blue Holly Hobbies holding a handful of wildflowers throughout. It was beautiful. So soft, so new, and so pretty. The front of the robe closed with pretend pearl buttons. It was the most beautiful robe I had ever seen. I never had new clothes bought for me. They were either hand-made from Gram or from the thrift store down the street.

This amazingly beautiful robe was the first new piece of clothing I remember ever owning, and it had my Holly all over it, which made it the best piece of clothing one could own.

I still had wished after I opened the gift that I had gotten Holly, but this was an awesome gift, too. I had totally forgotten the other gift and had gone into the bathroom to try my new robe on. The fit was perfect, and I felt like the belle of the ball. While I was changing, my aunt gave my brother a gift, a large metal truck, which he was playing with when I walked back into the room. I remember feeling like a princess with her new gown as I sat on the wood stairs and kept looking at the pearl buttons on my robe, wondering if they were real pearls.

Aunt May broke my train of thought. "Aren't you going to open the large gift Santa brought? The box was a large square — probably 18 inches square. It, too, was wrapped perfectly in bright red paper with a beautiful white bow. Aunt May again handed me the scissors, much like we were at a formal bow cutting, and once the bow was cut and the lid was off, I saw tons of tissue paper but nothing else. I dug through all the paper, not feeling anything at first, but then at the very bottom, I felt a cardboard package.

Please, please, please, I kept saying to myself as I cleared through all the tissue to see what was buried inside. As I pulled that last piece of tissue out of the box, I saw my Holly looking at me through the plastic window of her box, smiling at me like she was as happy to see me as I was to see her.

I was overjoyed by the moment. Santa had heard me. My voice counted. Someone cared enough to want me to be happy. I mattered. Both Aunt May *and* Santa cared about me. My heart brimmed with love, knowing that now that I have Holly, I won't be alone anymore. I knew she loved me back. It was one of the most special memories I have, Aunt May giving me this beautiful gift and my brother playing with his truck on the floor nearby. Me, feeling a love and acceptance unlike anything I had ever felt before. *I mattered to someone.* The thought was almost too much.

And then, the double-entendre, I mattered most to Holly. She was my responsibility now. I had to care for her and protect her. She was so much smaller than I, and she depended on me for everything. My Holly needed me to not only love her but also to keep her safe. That night before I fell asleep, I made her a promise. I promised that I would always love her and protect her forever and ever — all the while knowing full well there was no one to protect me.

For the next few days, Holly and I did everything together. I read her *Little House on the Prairie,* my favorite book, which I kept checking out of the school's library and had read at least five times. It was her favorite, too. She liked being read to, always smiling, and never making me feel bad when I mispronounced a word or lost my place. At night, when we went to bed and said prayers, I thanked God for giving her to me.

The first morning after Christmas break, I couldn't bear to leave her alone. I told Gram I was sick in a fake, scratchy voice. I even forced a few coughs. No luck. I tried to think of a way to sneak her to school with me, but I didn't have a backpack and had no way to carry her without being noticed. So, I carefully laid her on my bed and covered her, so no one would see her. I laid our favorite book next to her, so she wouldn't feel abandoned and said, "When I come back from school, I'll read you the next chapter."

Mom and David had been gone for days. They hadn't been at Gram's since the day after I brought Holly home. I loved when they weren't there, especially now that Holly was. I never missed them, but I did feel lonely and unwanted because I wasn't a part of anything or anyone's family. I was dumped at my Gram's, and I knew it. Gram did her best for me, but she had so much to deal with, and I felt like a burden to her.

School dragged that day. Minutes felt like hours, and hours felt like days as I watched the clock. Finally, the bell rang, and I ran to the bus, wanting to be home as soon as possible, thinking if I got to the bus super-fast, the bus would be able to leave and get me home sooner. Instead, we had to sit there for what seemed like forever, waiting for everyone to board. That entire day, all I thought about was Holly being alone and how scared she must have felt. I knew Gram was there in the morning when I left for school, but what if she had left to run errands? I knew how scary it was to be left alone because Mom had done it to me all the time.

The bus finally loaded and eventually dropped me at my stop, located at the top of our street. I got off the bus and ran as fast as I could down the hill toward Gram's house. Three-quarters of the way there, I could see the dead end, but I also saw Mom's car. My slow run turned into a sprint. I ran so hard my side hurt, but I didn't stop.

I ran upstairs to my room. I stopped dead in my tracks at the top of the stairs because my bedroom door, which I had closed, was now cracked open. I quickly pushed the door open, expecting to see David snooping through my stuff, but the room was empty. I turned my attention to my bed, where Holly had been tucked safely away and saw that the blankets had been tousled and not the way I left them. Immediately, I ran over and pulled them back. Panic and fear washed over me. Holly was gone. I pulled the blanket all the way down, searching for her, but she wasn't there.

For some reason, I was compelled to look under the bed. Nothing could have prepared me for what I saw. Scissors, a black pen, and pieces of what used to be beautiful yarn braids lay scattered. Farther back, Holly was lying on her stomach. I reached for her, far under the bed, feeling her arm. I pulled her toward me. I sat up and put her in my lap, tears running down my face and dropping onto hers. All of her braids had been cut off, and her beautiful face was now covered with black ink scribbles and fresh tears. Her patchwork dress was cut in places, and the ties to her bonnet had been cut off. I was horrified by what I saw. My poor Holly was almost unrecognizable with the graffiti on her sweet face.

My book was also a victim. It, too, was shoved under my bed with black scribbles throughout. Seeing all of the things I loved and cherished in front of me — now ruined — brought on an emotion I had never experienced. I had many emotions down pat: fear, humiliation, intimidation, embarrassment, and degradation. In the last week, I had learned joy and love. Once I experienced those, I was hooked. But this was a new emotion: rage. Rage was different. On this day, rage was introduced to my emotional palette. And it was powerful. It was *empowering*. For the first time ever, I had an emotion that trumped fear. This was the first day I took a stand against my mother — consequences be damned. I wasn't standing up for myself, though. If I were, fear would have won out. This was bigger than me. It was primal. It was, in a word, maternal.

I stood up with Holly's hand in my hand and stormed out of my room, down the stairs, and into the kitchen where both my mother and brother were. She was at the counter, making something to eat, and he was sitting at the table waiting.

With her back to me, I yelled, "Look what he did! He killed my Holly and ruined my book!"

Without turning around, she responded, "You should have put her away and not left your shit out." Still, with her back to me, she said, "Had you taken care of your toys, this would not have happened."

For a split second, I saw stars. Her assumption was so absurd, her tone so ridiculously callous. "I *did* take care of her *and* my book!" I screamed. "He did this on purpose, just like he always does. And you *always* let him."

She spun around so fast, I didn't have time to move. The back of her hand landed on the side of my face with a force so hard I fell to the ground. Tears ran down my cheeks, stinging as they rolled down my freshly raw skin. She grabbed my brother and walked out of the kitchen, through the front door to her car. As they walked past me, my brother flashed an evil smile, knowing he could get away with murder.

I ran to my room with my mutilated doll still clutched in my hand and threw myself on the bed, sobbing. "I am so sorry, Holly," I kept saying over and over. "I didn't protect you like I promised, and now you are gone, and I am alone again." I fell asleep crying and woke up hours later. My face was still throbbing, and I was in a daze. I went to the bathroom and looked into the mirror. I could hear Gram yelling something at Uncle Bobby, so I knew she was now home. I looked out of my bedroom window to see if my mother had returned. She hadn't, so I went downstairs because I was hungry. Gram was standing in the same place my mother had stood hours before, washing some pans with her back toward me.

"Is it dinner time? I asked.

"It's eight o'clock, and dinner is over. You slept through it and have to wait till breakfast." She turned around, the same as my mother did, not to hit me but to look at me to make her point that "sleeping your life away," as she called it, wasn't allowed. Then she saw my face. She asked hesitantly, "What happened to your face, Kim?"

But she knew. Seeing the fear and knowing in her eyes, I responded, "I must have slept on my hand." I turned to leave.

"Are you okay?" Her voice was quiet as we danced around the elephant in the room.

"Yes," I lied. "I just need to learn not to do it again."

She walked to the fridge and pulled out the leftover roast that had been for dinner.

"Get a plate," she said.

In silence, she put the leftovers on the table, and I sat to eat. She went up to her room and didn't come down for the rest of the night.

The next morning when I woke up, the sun seemed higher than usual. I jumped out of bed, knowing I had overslept and was late for the bus. I got dressed and went downstairs, wondering why Gram hadn't woken me. Gram was sitting at the kitchen table sipping coffee. She looked at me as I walked in.

"I'm keeping you home from school today," she told me. "After we do the chores this morning, I am going to take you out and buy you a new pair of shoes at Kinney's, and then we can have lunch at the diner."

This was music to my ears. I didn't want to go to school and have people look at me, see my face and make fun of it. My eyes were swollen and bloodshot from crying still, and the right side of my face still had the red outlines of my mother's fingers across my cheek. It didn't occur to me that that's why she was keeping me home.

My heart still ached, and I missed Holly. I felt responsible for what happened to her, and it made me hate myself even more than I did before. She was helpless, and she trusted me, and I failed her. All the love and joy I had felt was suddenly gone, replaced momentarily with rage, which had been beaten out of me with hate. All I had left were the painfully familiar emotions of humiliation, intimidation, embarrassment, degradation, and sadness — far too much for an eight-year-old to process.

Chapter 11

David and I were nothing alike. He was thin, with dark hair and dark eyes; he was the apple of my mother's eye. He was always getting into trouble and could never sit still. He could climb out of his crib by the time he was a year old and was always tearing stuff up. My mother never spanked him. Anything he tore up was my fault because I wasn't watching him or because I didn't put stuff out of his reach. He was four years younger than I but had my mother's mean streak. He saw how badly she treated me, so he did the same.

When I was seven, before moving to Gram's, he had found a hammer and chased me around, trying to hit me with it. All the while, my mother laughed, egging him on to "get her," which he did. The hammer landed in the middle of my back. She laughed, he laughed, and I cried. I was always afraid of him, and controlling him was impossible. He never listened to me and would hit me, bite me, and pull my hair if I got in his way. As he got older, his behavior got worse. He never listened to Gram when they would come over. He would steal things from my uncle Bobby's room and break them.

My mother protected him. She gave him every bit of loving attention she had and took him out for ice cream or to the movies — always without me. The only time I was included was when my aunts and cousins came over. I would be included, but only to save face, not because she wanted me there.

The summer I was ten, my mother had a part-time job working at the local elementary school kitchen. One day, she left David with Gram and me while she was at work. We were sent outside to play. There was a family that lived a few houses up from us. They had three older girls and a boy who was David's age. His name was Louis, and he was playing outside as well. He had a golf club that he must have taken from his father's golf bag in the garage, and he was swinging it, pretending to golf with rocks.

One of his sisters, Vivian, was close to my age and was also outside, playing hopscotch at the dead end. She and I often played together, and when I saw that she was out, I joined her and told David to go play with Louis, who was still swinging at rocks with the golf club. David walked over and proceeded to take the club away from him. Louis resisted, but David kept grabbing for the club. Eventually, he pushed Louis down on the ground, so he could take it. I heard the fighting and tried to break it up. Louis got up off the ground and reached for his club. David swung it and hit him across the chest. By now, Vivian had run and gotten her mother. The two of them came back to the fight and saw what my brother had done. They started screaming at him and pulled the club out of his hands.

David, in a rage, yelled back, "I'm going to tell my mother on you!"

I pulled him away from the scene. Terrified of what my mother would do to me if she found out what happened, I said, "Let's go home. I will buy you an ice cream when the ice cream man comes. I won't tell Mom." I was hoping he would think I was protecting him and not me. He calmed down.

We got back to Gram's house and hadn't been inside for more than two minutes when there was a pounding at the door. My heart sank. My mother wasn't home, but she would be soon, and I didn't want her to know that again, I didn't do my job.

I hid myself in a small closet under the stairs, my best hiding place. My brother was lying on the living room floor watching TV — oblivious. The pounding continued. Gram was in the garden and couldn't hear it, so I stayed hidden, hoping Louis' mom would leave. But then I heard a loud upset voice and another voice outside the front door. And then the door opened. I cracked open the closet door, so I could watch. Gram screamed for David, "Come outside right now!" she said.

He ignored her like he always did, even though he could clearly hear her. Neighbors down the street could hear her; she was so loud. The door swung open, light flooded in, and only the shape of Louis and his mom were visible from where I was hidden. Gram burst into the front room again, calling for David, enraged that he hadn't responded, and pulled him from where he was watching TV.

"What did you do? Did you hit Louis?" she barked.

He tried to get away from the clutch of her hand around his arm as they made their way outside, where poor Louis and his mom were standing. Louis was still crying. His mother wanted justice so much that she was willing to ignore her son, who was visibly hurt. He was clearly defeated and wished he weren't standing on our front porch. I knew this feeling all too well and felt so sorry for him. It occurred to me at that moment that bullies are drawn to those of us who just enjoy a simple thing without worrying about what someone thinks. But bullies see that joy and try to take it away from the person. They never try to just enjoy their own simple things. They either try to make what we enjoy seem worthless or — more drastically — do what my brother did: try to take the thing that they are enjoying and use it as a weapon to hurt them because they are jealous, not for the thing, but for the joy the thing brings them. Even though this had been the story of my entire life, seeing it happen to someone else made me realize that things like that didn't happen only to me.

Now Gram had my brother outside. I heard more loud voices, more crying from both boys, one in real pain and the other trying to cry his way out of trouble. And then it got quieter. I still heard David crying as they came back inside, but Louis and his mom had left.

I came out of my hiding spot to see Gram sitting on the sofa, my brother bent over her lap, pants down, and she was spanking him. He howled and cried like he was dying. And then the front door burst open. There I stood, out of my hiding place, watching Gram spank David. He had never been spanked before, and I was just trying to take it in. Then Mom walked through the front door. She ran over and pulled my brother away from his much-deserved punishment, screaming at Gram.

"What the hell is going on?" Mom demanded.

Gram started to tell her what had happened and that he needed to be punished. But then Mom saw me cowering in the corner, so close to my hiding spot. She glared at me, her blue eyes piercing and filled with loathing, letting me know this was all my fault and that I was going to pay.

She turned toward Gram, yelling," If you ever touch my son again, it will be the last time." And with that, she grabbed me by the hair and dragged me to the back room where she and David slept.

Anger and hatred filled her eyes as she pushed me onto the bed.

"I told you to watch your brother!" she screamed. "Roll over!"

"No, mommy! Please!" I pleaded. "I tried, but he wouldn't listen. He hit me with the club, too, when I tried to stop him."

"Roll over!" she screamed.

I didn't. I was scared and didn't want the belt again. "Please don't hit me," I begged as I tried to wriggle away. She was trying to roll me onto my stomach. She grabbed my hair, pulled me off the bed, twisted me around, and pushed me back onto the bed, face down. She pulled down my shorts and panties with her free hand and took the belt that was always close by and started hitting me, the clutch of my hair never released, my feet still planted on the floor. The pain was so bad all I could do was scream. Then the door of the bedroom flew open, and Gram's voice screamed, "Stop!"

And she did.

Time slowed down. The next swing of the belt didn't come. Gram stood at the bedroom door. The belt fell to the floor. Mom released her clutch of my hair. She pivoted, and in a split second, the hand that had been holding the belt was now swinging a clenched fist at Gram's face, knocking her almost off her feet. Gram let out a gasp and a throaty cry, the sound one makes when the pain is too much to bear. Her pain came as much from within as from the blow to her throbbing face. I was filled with guilt, shame, and fear.

"Don't hurt Gram because I didn't do what I was supposed to!" I screamed. "It's not her fault, Mommy. I'm sorry, I will do better. Please!"

My mother's mouth twisted like she had tasted the most vile thing in the world, her eyes burning into my face like the red butt of the cigarette she had burned me with so many times. "You both are made for each other," she spewed. "She is a nagging battle ax, and you are a worthless piece of shit!"

She stormed out of the room and out to her car. Her tires squealed as she drove away. I crawled onto the bed, lying on my stomach because my backside hurt so bad. My panties and shorts were still around my ankles as I buried my face in the pillow and sobbed. My mind played over and over what had just happened, seeing the look on Gram's face when she tried to stop my mom, who spewed hate and disgust with every swing of her arm. I saw Gram with tears rolling down her face and heard the guttural sobs as she came to terms with the monster she had created.

"It's all my fault. I made this happen," I kept saying to myself, through my sobs, into the pillow until, at last, I fell asleep.

When I woke up later that evening, the sun had set, and the room was dark. I slowly got off the bed, feeling the welts on my backside with every move. *I can't go out there*, I thought to myself. *I don't want to see Gram.* I was so full of shame because what happened to her was my fault. My panties and shorts still at my feet, I tried to pull them up, but it hurt so much that I slowly took my legs out and stood in the dark room half-naked, not knowing what to do. I didn't want to be in this room.

My mother could be back at any time. But if I left the room, I would see Gram, and she probably hated me for what happened to her. Just then, the door opened, the light from the hall flooding the dark room with me standing half-naked in the middle. I jumped back in surprise, my welts reminding me they were still there as I did, and saw Gram standing in the doorway. She had my Holly robe in her hand and handed it to me.

"Here. Put this on. Don't worry about panties tonight. You can sleep in your robe," she said.

I couldn't look at her face, afraid of what I would see.

"Once you're covered, come out of this room. Dinner is ready." She didn't sound mad or like she did when my mother hit her. She sounded like Gram, and I was able to breathe a little easier. Once I had my robe on, I went into the kitchen where she had made my favorite — spaghetti with butter and shake cheese. I still couldn't look at her, but I took my bowl of pasta toward the kitchen table, dreading having to sit on the hard chair. My uncle was in the kitchen as well. She gave him his bowl of pasta and then announced, "Tonight, we get to eat in the living room and watch TV."

This was never allowed. Sometimes my uncle would sneak food and lie on his stomach and watch TV until he got caught. So when Gram announced this, he was thrilled. "Thanks, Ma!" he said with a big smile, so pure and happy.

I followed him into the living room with Gram behind us. And as he did many times before, lay on his stomach with his bowl in front of him, his elbows propping him up as he ate. I lay on my belly and ate my pasta, feeling thankful that I didn't have to sit, but still afraid to look Gram in the face. We watched *Barnaby Jones* on the TV in silence until bedtime. I was exhausted and didn't mind going to bed at all. Plus, I wanted to be in bed before my mother came back — if she came back.

After I washed my dish in the sink, I saw Gram still sitting on the sofa, but now the room was dark except for the light from the hall. I was surprised, and seeing her sitting in a dark room in silence scared me. She hated dark rooms and was always opening blinds to let light in. For the first time since Mom had stormed out, I was brave enough to look up at her. She was still sitting on the sofa, but now she was staring out the window, not looking over at me when I came in. Heavy sadness and silence filled the room. I stood there for a minute looking at her profile, her hands twisting at the end of an afghan that lay across her lap.

"'Night, Gram," I managed to mutter, the words so large I could hardly get them out of my mouth. What I wanted to say was, "I am so sorry, Gram. It's all my fault. Please don't hate me. I will do better next time, I promise." But I wasn't brave enough. I was afraid that she would confirm everything I thought of myself if I let her know how I felt. She continued to stare out the window. I didn't wait for a response. I felt like the failure I had always been told I was. As I approached the stairs, out of the darkness, she said, "I love you." The words stopped me in my tracks.

"I love you, too, Gram," I replied instantly.

My heart was lightened by her words. Both of us had experienced heartbreak that day, both feeling like we failed the other, both wishing we could have stopped it to protect the other. As I headed up the stairs, I turned to look back to where she sat. I could see her silhouette on the sofa. The moon was accommodating that night, shining in through the front window, and I saw her face. Tears rolled down her cheeks, with no tissue to stop or hide them. The sight of her pain hurt me way more than the welts left on my backside. I hated myself for having caused such pain to someone who loved me. And when I reached the top of the stairs, I said out loud, but not loud enough, "I'm sorry, Gram. It's my fault."

Chapter 12

Mom came and went often in these years. When she was gone, life was easy. Go to school, do chores, go to the Kingdom Hall, go door to door to witness with Gram, and play outside. When Mom came, she had no interest in spending time with me. We really didn't even speak to each other. She would show up, or her car would be in front of the house when I came home from school, and she would leave without saying goodbye. This was fine for me because the house felt unsafe when she was there.

Usually, I played with neighborhood kids, mostly boys, at the end of our block, but what I really wanted was a friend, a girlfriend that wanted to do girl things. My mother had always kept my hair short, and Gram cut my bangs crooked. I longed just to look like a girl and would have loved to be pretty. I wanted a girl to be my friend, and then we'd hang around together, like the girls I saw on the bus — sitting, laughing together. In my imagination, my hair was long and pulled back into cute braids, or I'd wear a bow.

In fifth grade, I became friends with the girl who lived at the top of my street. Her name was Kathy. She was like the girls in my imagination. Her hair was long and curled in ringlets. She wore pretty dresses and new, black, patent-leather Mary Janes. Her mother had died a few months prior from picking at a mole on her back, and her dad traveled for work and was never home, so she was left to be raised by her gram like me. Our friendship started when I was playing kickball with the gang at the end of the block. She rode her three-speed bike to the end of the block and invited me to come over the next day to see her new record player. I was thrilled.

We started to hang out almost every Saturday and Sunday. We would sit in the carport and listen to 45s on her portable record player and play gin rummy.

Kathy wasn't much like me, though, other than her living arrangement. In addition to being pretty, with long wavy hair, she was petite and not chubby. I was the opposite: taller than anyone in my grade and chunky. She got to take piano lessons and wear new, stylish clothes that her dad would buy for her when he was in town. Her gram always catered to her, and she never had to work in the garden or pick blackberries and be scratched with the thorns — or do any chores for that matter. Yet we were both alone, abandoned for different reasons — though reasons don't matter when you are a child. We had both lost a parent to death and felt unwanted, in the way, and not good enough for our remaining parent to be with us. Kathy and I spent many days looking at her *Tiger Beat* magazines, which almost always had pictures of Shawn Cassidy, who we both had crushes on.

We were friends on weekends and during the summer but not at school. At school, she pretended she didn't know me and hung out with the popular girls. It was like our friendship was a secret. Because we had fun and got along so well, it never occurred to me that she might be embarrassed by me. It was almost like a game. She would ignore me during school and on the bus, but once we got off the bus, she was my friend, acting normally. I was so desperate to have a friend I played along, not caring that she ignored me in front of other kids.

One day, I saw the latest *Tiger Beat* magazine at Woolworth's, and Shawn Cassidy was on the front cover. I couldn't wait to tell Kathy at school. I was so excited that when I saw her at lunch, sitting with Vivian, the most popular girl in the sixth grade, I stopped and excitedly told her the news. Her reaction was not what I had expected. I knew I had broken the unspoken rule of not talking at school, but it was *Shawn Cassidy!* She was visibly embarrassed and uncomfortable. She didn't say a word to me. Then Vivian leaned in and whispered something to her, and they both started to laugh.

Being made fun of is especially horrible when it's done by your best and only friend. My heart broke. Suddenly, I felt isolated, used, and betrayed. I thought I was important, like a real friend, not just a convenience. That was the last time we spoke. When I went to her house to hang out the next day, her gram told me she was busy. I went every day for a week after school and on the weekend to see if she could hang out. Each time her gram met me at the door saying, "Sorry dear, she's busy."

I was crushed. I couldn't understand what I had done that was so wrong to make her shut me out of her life completely. Now we weren't friends at school *or* at home. She wouldn't even look at me as we waited at the bus stop in the mornings. With the other kids, I was used to feeling rejected because of how I looked, what I wore, and my not being able to celebrate holidays or salute the flag in class. But I thought she and I understood each other and that somehow, our circumstances and shared pain and loneliness were stronger than our social status in school. I learned that year that no one wants others to know life has dealt you a shit sandwich — that you're broken and unwanted — even if it's true.

This happened at the end of sixth grade. Mom and David had now permanently moved into Gram's house. Things had gotten a little better since she hit Gram in the face. The beatings slowed down to about twice a month instead of a few times a week, and they only happened when Gram wasn't home. Mom would scream at me as she whipped me that I would understand when I was an adult. And then she'd tell me she would put me in a home for bad kids if I said anything.

"This is your fault," she'd say. "That mouth of yours will be the death of you someday."

During this period, I watched her frequently steal money from Gram's purse. Once, she caught me watching while she did it and glared at me with a threatening look. It was the same look I got every time I had to pull my pants down for the belt. I never said anything. Her threats were real, and I didn't want my mouth to be the death of me.

Chapter 13

That same year, Mom got a boyfriend. She and David would leave to go to his house a lot, and David would play with Ray, his son. David told me all about it, but I didn't know or meet either of them for months. Just after Christmas, Mom told me to go upstairs and clean up. It was late afternoon during Christmas break, and she and David had been gone all day. I had spent the day reading a Nancy Drew book.

"Where are we going?" I asked, not wanting to go.

"We have been invited to dinner, and Ben wants to meet you," she said, as though this were a normal thing — anyone wanting to meet me *and* her telling me about it. She never boasted about me, so there was never any reason anyone would want to meet me. And even if they did, she would never let me know that because it would "go to my head."

"Who's Ben?" I asked, wondering how he even knew about me.

This was the first time she had mentioned his name. Even though she hadn't said much, I felt uncomfortable with not just what she said, but that she had said it. There wasn't a single insult in her solitary sentence to me, and her voice had no bite. She was being *nice*. It was unnatural, odd. I had never felt love of any kind from my mother. Not in her words, nor her actions, ever. I never heard her say "I love you" or even "I like you." She hadn't said anything positive to me in my eleven years of life. No hugs, no "great job," no "I'm proud of you." And more important, I never *felt* love, like, or even tolerance from her. But now she was telling me someone *wanted* to meet me. This felt wrong. Her actions were a lie like she was up to something. Despite my wariness, I begrudgingly got ready, dreading what lay ahead of me.

We arrived at Ben's apartment about an hour later. He lived on the second floor of a nice complex. When he opened the door, I noticed his salt-and-pepper, slicked-back hair, the smell of aftershave, and music playing in the background. He stood in front of us, one hand holding the door open, the other holding a crystal glass with red wine in it.

"Welcome," he said and smiled, opening the door so we could enter.

He seemed so put together. He wore a pressed, light-green shirt and jeans that had been pressed as well. His apartment was neat and clean. His decorating was way more modern than Gram's. He had only one TV, with no foil on the antenna, and a large collection of balsa model airplanes along one wall. For some reason, I couldn't understand why my mother was here, let alone that she had been here before. She was the exact opposite of this. She was unkempt, didn't clean anything, and had no style or creative hobbies.

As I watched how she interacted with Ben, I kept thinking to myself, *Who is this person?* She was nice and smiling, and she did the dishes after dinner. *This is not my mother,* I kept thinking to myself. My brother and Ben's son were busy playing with a Light Bright, so I just watched this very unfamiliar night unfold. My mother seemed normal, happy. She addressed me in non-hateful ways the entire night, which put me on edge. *Who was she pretending to be?* Somehow, the night ended peacefully, and to my bewilderment, nothing bad came of it.

I went to Ben's for dinner a few more times. He would always have Marty Robbins or Johnny Cash playing in the background, dressed in a pressed, short-sleeve shirt, his graying hair slicked back neat, and he smelled like a blend of Marlboro cigarettes and Old Spice. The dinners were always nice, but I felt like I was in the way. My mother spent her time trying to impress Ben and make him love her. I could see through her fakeness as I watched her be kind and neat and pretend that this was who she actually was.

She would buy him an expensive gift every time we went over and have him open it after dinner like it was his birthday. Model plane kits, expensive bottles of scotch, a watch he had mentioned he wanted, and a leather bomber jacket. My brother and Ray would get a new toy to play with each time we went over, too. They spent their time together playing with, breaking, or fighting over the toy after dinner in Ray's room.

I didn't get gifts, nor did I get to play after dinner. My job was to clear the table and do the dishes. The second time we went to dinner at Ben's, we had stopped at the mall on the way.

"Can I get a book to take over?" I asked, hoping she would be nice like she pretended to be when we were at Ben's apartment.

"Be grateful I'm even bringing you," she snapped in front of the cashier.

No book for me that day. No gifts. Just a healthy dose of humiliation. After dinner and after I had finished the dishes, I was playing solitaire on the floor when I heard her call my name.

"Kim! Get back in this kitchen!"

When I walked in, she was holding a skillet I had washed.

"Look at this pan. It's filthy!" She shoved it toward me.

I looked at it, and it seemed clean to me, and I stated this in a quiet manner so that Ben couldn't hear us in the living room.

"Touch it!" She continued loudly. "It's filthy and covered in grease!"

I took my finger and ran it across the pan. She was right. The pan looked clean but was still greasy.

"I want you to rewash every dish right now," she said and filled the sink with scalding water. I reached in for the sponge but quickly pulled my hand back out. "It's too hot," I said.

"I want every dish rewashed," she said. She took my hand and shoved it into the scalding water. Just then, Ben walked into the kitchen to get another glass of Paul Mason wine.

"What's going on?" he asked.

"Kim's rewashing the dishes because she did a shitty job."

Tears of pain and humiliation ran down my face. My hand was still in the burning water. I was afraid of what she would do if I pulled it out. He looked at me in a stern way and said, "If you do something, you should always do it right the first time."

I wanted to die; I was so embarrassed and humiliated. *He thinks I am a failure, too.* That's what kept running through my head. He wasn't trying to be cruel, and he was right. What hurt the most was that he had seen what I had tried so desperately to hide: that I was an imperfect, unwanted child. I knew this was true because my mother reminded me of it on a daily basis.

I quickly rewashed the dishes, making sure they were grease-free, my hands beet red from the heat of the water. I went into the bathroom and ran them under cold water until the redness faded, and then I went back into the dining room, where they were playing cards.

"I'm done," I told her, not making eye contact with either of them. I went to the living room, where my interrupted game of solitaire waited for my return.

"Let's check and make sure they are spotless," she said before I could sit down. Back to the kitchen, I went, hoping and praying I did a better job as I watched her check every dish in the dish drying rack, not wanting to be embarrassed and humiliated again.

After she checked each dish thoroughly, she said, "This is how they should have been done the first time." I was dismissed.

By this time, I was emotionally drained and wished I were back home with Gram. I quickly turned around and walked back again to my incomplete card game. Halfway there, I heard my mother say something to me that stopped me dead.

"You know I love you, right?"

In disbelief of what I had heard for the first time ever from her, I turned around and saw her standing next to Ben, who was sitting at the kitchen table. Both were looking at me, waiting for my reply. *No, I don't know you love me. How could I? You beat me, you burn me with your cigarette and laugh, and every day I hear how I was a mistake and should have been aborted.* I stood there with no voice for what seemed like an hour instead of seconds. Finally, I replied, "Yes." It was the answer they both had waited to hear. I had waited my whole life to hear those words.

Just then, there was a loud crash in the bedroom where the boys had been playing, and the attention was taken off me, thank God. The rest of the evening turned into a large argument because my brother had been playing with model airplanes that he wasn't supposed to be touching and broke one. Typical behavior from my brother. Never did he have boundaries set or discipline when he did something wrong. I was the scapegoat every time. Except tonight. He did something he wasn't supposed to do, and Ben thought he should be disciplined, and my mother disagreed. She made excuses about David not having a father figure and that it wasn't his fault really because he had no role model, all bullshit reasons she could drum up to protect him.

This was the first of many arguments that revolved around my brother and his behavior. Ben's son was a quiet child, used to playing on his own and always being held accountable for his actions. Ben was a rule follower, practical and fair, but he had the "Do as you say, say as you do" mentality. He was the complete opposite of my mother. No wonder she was showering him with gifts and attention; she knew he was way out of her league and used whatever she could to try to get him to love her.

Chapter 14

A couple months later, during a dinner at Ben's, the conversation of him moving to Kansas came up. This was the first time I had heard of him moving. I knew Mom would not be happy about this. Everything she did revolved around trying to make him love her. I had overheard him tell her once, straight up, that he cared for her but didn't want to be more serious than that. So in a nice way, he was saying, "I don't love you," but she continued to press the issue. With him relocating, she would be back to her real self. And she'd be back to focusing on what ruined her life: me, because all hope of getting Ben to love her was now clearly out the door. I dreaded this return to normal. Despair set in as I braced myself for what I knew was coming next.

A week later, my mother made an announcement. "We're moving," she said as she leaned against the kitchen counter. "The guy who killed Ritchie is getting out of prison in June, and we need to leave." It was the end of April. Apparently, she had received death threats against her and needed to get as far away as possible. "We're going to Arizona, and I'll find a job in Flagstaff. It's not as hot there as it is in Phoenix."

When I walked out of the kitchen, I felt happy. She was leaving. No more beatings, no more verbal abuse, finally. But I was wrong — horrifically wrong.

Over the next two weeks, my mother spent every moment at Ben's house. One day, Gram and I were pulling weeds in the yard. Out of the blue, she said to me, "You have to go with your mother, Kim. She is your mother, and you need to be with her."

Her words hit me as hard as my mother's belt.

"I don't want to go, Gram. Why can't I stay with you?" I said, confused and perplexed. "Please let me stay. I promise I will be good, Gram!"

She wouldn't look at me as I begged.

"She is your mother, and she wants to take you with her. Maybe you should go and live with her. She is your mother. I'm not," she said.

My heart broke. To me, Gram was my mom, and I loved her as if she were. She kept me safe and made sure I had what I needed to be okay. She took a hit from her own daughter trying to protect me. And I thought she felt the same way until that day. I felt like I didn't belong anywhere. Gram didn't want me, Mom was taking me away, and Gram was letting her. I knew there was a reason my mother wanted me to go with her. It wasn't because she loved me; that I was sure of. Maybe she was trying to hurt Gram just as she had when she kept me and didn't give me up for adoption. She had power over my grandfather back then, and now she had power over Gram the same way. I didn't understand. I felt abandoned, scared, and alone.

The next few weeks flew by. My mother was at Ben's house most of the time, still trying to get him to love her, wanting him to ask her to move to Kansas with him. I knew this because when she wasn't at his apartment, she was on the phone with him, and I heard her conversations. But he didn't invite her, and she was now committed to starting a new life in Arizona. She was crafty and planned our move at the same time as Ben's, saying that we could follow him to Kansas and then drive to Arizona, still hoping he would change his mind. She rented a U-Haul and loaded up her few possessions.

Most of the furniture from the shack we lived in was broken, dirty junk, so we just left it behind. The buyer wanted the property and planned to demolish the shack and garage to build a new beautiful house instead. She arranged for David to stay with my aunt, saying he was too young for the drive, but the truth was Ben didn't care for

David, and my mother's chances of changing Ben's mind during the three-day drive would be much lower if my brother were around. Even though it wasn't permanent, I could tell that she and Ben got along better without David underfoot.

The day we left was like a bad dream. I had been hoping that Gram would stand up and tell my mother she couldn't take me, that I belonged with her, that I was hers. But she didn't. In the middle of the afternoon on a Saturday, the day we were supposed to leave, Gram sat on a bench swing that she had in the front yard, just staring off somewhere, but definitely not at the grass in front of her. I had spent the morning sitting on my bed, hoping that things would somehow change. That I could stay here, in my home, and not go. *Who will protect me?* I kept asking myself. I begged God not to let this happen. I heard the moving truck pull up, the engine turn off, and the door shut. My mother came in soon after, yelling for me up the stairs.

"Let's go, Kim! Get down here. We need to go."

Again, I begged God, *Please let me stay,* and hesitantly got off my bed and headed downstairs. Mom was smoking on the front porch; Gram was still sitting on the porch swing under the large birch tree in the front yard. As I walked onto the porch, I saw her still staring into space, her face blank with expression, just as it was when I looked out of my window hours earlier. I walked up toward her, wishing she would look at me, but she didn't. I leaned down and gave her a hug. Still, she didn't acknowledge my presence.

"Bye, Gram," I said as I hugged her. "I love you."

No response. It was like her body sat in the middle of this swing, but her spirit was somewhere else. She never said goodbye that day. She didn't say a word and didn't look at me as I walked past her. *Please say something,* I thought to myself as I walked down the sidewalk and reached the tall trees that blocked the truck I dreaded getting into. I turned around one more time with the hopes that she was coming

87

toward me to stop this from happening, but instead, she just sat on the swing, with tears running down her solemn face.

I knew at that moment she wasn't stopping this from happening. She didn't know how. And as I walked past the tall trees, I said in a quiet voice, "I love you, Gram, and will miss you." Seeing her like this broke my heart, and I wanted her to know I was going to be okay, even though I knew that was a lie.

We headed out of town, following Ben and Ray. Ben had rented a smaller U-Haul than ours and hitched his truck to the back. Mom cried a lot in the car, and when a certain song came on the radio, she cried even more. I tried to sleep as much as I could. I didn't want to think about what was happening; the uncertainty of my future scared me. Her crying scared me as well.

I think this was the first time I saw my mother feel something besides rage, anger, and annoyance. This was her third face. The first was the abusive, hateful face, the second was the one she wore when she was around my aunts and cousins. It was more of a "feel sorry for me" face or a "fun aunt who played in the community pool when my cousins came to visit" face. And then there was this face, the face of heartbreak. The face that knew all of her coercion didn't work and the man in the smaller U-Haul in front of us didn't want her — at least, not enough to ask her to move with him to Kansas.

I felt sorry for her but had no idea what to say or do. So I kept my eyes shut most of the way to Kansas except for when we stopped for gas breaks, lunch, and the Howard Johnson Motel for the evening that first night. Ray and I shared a room, and Mom and Ben shared the other. After eating dinner, Ray and I got to go to the outside pool and swim. It was awesome. We swam way past dark, with neither parent there to supervise, but I didn't care. I looked at my torso and legs in the pool, wishing they were as slim as they looked in the water.

Ray and I finally went back to our room when the pool closed, and a man in a navy jumpsuit turned the lights out and started to close the chain-link gate. We got into the room, not really saying much to each other. He was four years younger than I but very disciplined, so he immediately went to the bathroom to change and brush his teeth and then crawled into bed. I did the same after he had finished, but instead of going to sleep, I settled into bed with my latest Nancy Drew mystery. This was my escape on any given painful day. I read and pretended the life, mystery, and extraordinary, always pretty and popular person I was reading about was mine and me, because it was so very much nicer than my real life, my misery, and the real me — the unwanted, ugly mistake.

We made it to Kansas the next evening and found the home that Ben had rented. The sun was just starting to set, so he invited us to stay the night. We unloaded his small moving truck and set up his and Ray's beds. Mom and Ben started drinking Paul Mason wine, and Ray and I went to bed. Ray in his room in his bed, and me on a blanket in the living room. I could hear Mom and Ben talking in the dining room. She was crying, saying how much she wished she could stay here with him, and him reminding her that it was best for her to go to Arizona and start her new life, in a calm, matter-of-fact way. I drifted off soon after, not looking forward to what was ahead, knowing that he wasn't going to give in and have us stay, knowing that once away from him, she would be the person I was used to, because she didn't have to pretend anymore. *She'll be worse,* I thought to myself, *I just know it. She will blame me for this.* I had never lived with her by myself before, and I was scared. I missed Gram and my home and just wanted to go back where I could be safe.

We left the next day, goodbyes said and long, tear-filled hugs given.

"I love you," she said.

"Drive safe," he replied.

I felt bad for her but hurried up and got in the truck, so I didn't have to see the rejection and her distraught face as she hugged him. The drive to Arizona was much like the drive to Kansas but worse. She cried most of the way and talked to herself about how he didn't deserve her, that he was an old man and she could do so much better.

Years later, I realized that this move had nothing to do with the man who murdered Ritchie. It dawned on me that she made up the story of being in danger in hopes that Ben would stay with her.

Chapter 15

When we got to Arizona, we stayed for two weeks with Aunt Thelma, who had moved there because she had breathing issues, during which time Mom spent no time looking for jobs. She partied with her cousin Joe, who was a junkie, and she called Ben every night to tell him there were no jobs and that she felt unsafe.

"What if those bad people who killed Ritchie find me and do something horrible to me, or worse, to Kim?" she said, as if my safety were ever her priority.

David was still in Connecticut, staying with my aunt. Finally, Ben gave in.

"Come here, and find a job and a place," he said. "But it's temporary — just till you get your own place. That way you can be safe." At least that's what she said when she came into the room I had been sleeping in.

"We are leaving in the morning, so make sure you have all your stuff packed," she told me.

The next morning, we headed back to Kansas. Her mood had swung 180 degrees. She was once again the nice person she pretended to be in front of Ben. At least, that's what I thought.

We reached Kansas in record time, not even staying overnight in a hotel. She pulled off the highway and napped for a few hours in Albuquerque and made it to Kansas in less than a day.

We took the first few days to settle in and fly my brother out. For the next few weeks, everything was new and good. I enrolled in seventh grade in the junior high down the street from Ben's house, and David and Ray went to the elementary school across the main road from where Ben lived. There wasn't much talk of Mom finding a home or a job or moving, so I thought maybe we were staying.

Two months passed, and the shine of all things new and good had worn off. Ben and Mom fought a lot, mainly because David wasn't being controlled or held accountable for his actions. After three months, the fighting was worse. They called each other names, slammed doors, drank a lot, and had fights that lasted for days.

One night, David got into Ray's room and broke his favorite telescope. I felt so bad for Ray, remembering my poor Holly Hobbie and what he had done to her. Ray came out of his room crying to Ben, clutching part of the broken telescope in his hand. The drinking had started early that evening, and Ben had had enough. He took the broken piece and slammed it on the kitchen counter, breaking it even more. I had been sitting in the living room watching *Mork and Mindy*. I heard the crash and got up to see what was going on, just in time to see Ray's face as his telescope got even more broken. He was horrified at his dad's outburst and that there had been even more damage to his favorite thing. Mom started to scream back at Ben, accusing him of playing favorites and not treating my brother the same as Ray. The fight got really hot after that. Ben told my mother the horrible truths about David, who was now standing right beside her, with a smug look on his face. He was untouchable, and he knew it. Ben was so angry; his ears were red and his face stone cold.

"You're a lazy bitch," Ben said as he stood up from his chair. "And your son is a menace to society." He walked across the room to the bar. "This is my house!" he roared as he poured another drink from the crystal decanter and lit another Marlboro.

Mom jumped up and stood two inches from him, her own highball of Jack Daniels dangling from her fingertips. Glaring, she replied with venom, "Don't you dare call my son a menace. Your son is a weak pussy who cries to get whatever he wants, and you're a pussy to give it to him."

Ben turned to Ray. "Hit him," Ben said.

Ray was much smaller than my brother and didn't have the mean streak in him like David did. A look of horror washed over Ray's face.

"Hit him, I said!" Ben roared. "Stand up for yourself!"

More out of fear of what his father thought of him or would do to him than out of his anger at my brother, Ray gave David a push. I think he hoped that would appease Ben, and he could go back to his room and try to forget this horrible incident. But nope. Instead, this pissed Mom off, and she finally showed Ben and Ray her true colors.

The real person I knew screamed at David, "Kick his ass!"

And David proceeded to do just that. Ben yelled at Ray to fight back, and Ray tried, but David's spirit was much more aggressive and violent. Every time Ray tried to retaliate, my brother came at him three times worse. I stood there, watching two adults prodding their children to beat the shit out of each other right in front of me. David hit Ray so hard that he cried out in pain and stopped trying to fight back. Mom cheered.

"Go to your room, and stop your fucking blubbering," Ben said to Ray, full of disgust.

Poor Ray, I thought over and over again. But I never stepped in to help him. I should have, but I wasn't brave enough. I was also embarrassed by the whole situation and felt relieved that it wasn't me this time.

That was the night I knew we had to leave.

The next day, my mother found a house for sale and made an offer. We moved in a couple weeks later, but those weeks at Ben's were full of silence, hatred, and awkward discomfort. Despite how unpleasant it was at Ben's, I hated that we had to go. Living with Ben was the closest I ever got to a normal family situation. Ben was nice to me — distant but nice. And there had been no beatings or verbal abuse for a few months.

During this time, Mom had made a few attempts to smooth things over with Ben, but he hardly looked at her. He stopped at the bar every night after work. On the weekends, he left early with Ray and didn't come home till after dark. I never asked Ray where they went. I didn't want to know. A couple of times Mom tried to follow them, leaving before they did, saying she had to go to the store, but then she'd park down the street and wait for them to leave. She was never able to follow them successfully, though. She had a yellow 1970 Ford Galaxy that stood out in a crowd. I know she did this because she took David and me with her.

"You'd better not say a word, or it will be the last word you ever say," she threatened.

Of course, she never threatened David. I knew she'd go back to her old ways and that she may actually be worse now because she was even more miserable than ever. I was scared.

Chapter 16

The house my mother purchased was an 800-square-foot, single-story track house with two bedrooms and one bath. I didn't see it until we pulled up in our moving truck the day we moved in. It was late fall before Thanksgiving. The whole house was a horrible, medium shade of blue, even the trim. It was built in the 1940s and looked like every other house on the block, except more run-down. As I lugged my suitcase through the tiny living room, I asked which room was mine.

"You and your brother are sharing," she said.

My heart sank. Not only did I despise my brother, but I was nearly 13 and fully developed. I had started my period over the summer, and the thought of sharing my room with him hit me like a ton of bricks. Even though he was only eight, he was just as abusive as my mother, and I didn't trust him at all.

"I want to go back to Gram's," I said. "I hate it here! You don't want me here anyways!"

I said it too loudly, like a person who was trying to find her voice, a person who so wanted to be brave enough to stand up for herself. But in the heat of the moment, I forgot that I wasn't strong and would bear the repercussions for my outburst. She did not disappoint. Just minutes after arriving at our new house, I was greeted with a backhand to my face, and it was my not-so-gentle reminder that I didn't have a voice and that trying to find it would be painful.

Ben didn't help with the move, so my buffer was gone. I was on my own, and I had never felt more alone than at that moment. I sensed that things would be worse than before, but I was still full of uncertainty about what was in store. I had only spoken to Gram once since we left Connecticut. It was a long-distance toll call, and we'd had to use Ben's phone. Now we didn't even have that.

I thought starting a new school in the middle of seventh grade would make me stand out like a sore thumb, but the town was so small that it wouldn't have mattered when I started. It was just outside of Wichita, and it was one of those towns where most of the people who lived there had been born there, and the rest of my class had known each other since kindergarten. They also knew one another from church or Girl Scouts. There was no hiding my newcomer status. It felt like everyone's attention was on me, and they had all banded together to not let me into their little club.

I was used to not fitting in, so I just went to school every day, and during class, I would daydream that my father would find me. My mother had told me that he left when he found out she was pregnant and didn't want anything to do with me or her. She said that he joined the military to get away from me and didn't want me. I had asked her about him on our way to Kansas from Connecticut. I was hoping she would tell me something good, something positive that I could hold onto. I had never really wondered about him until then.

Maybe that was because I was just so busy trying to survive my mother, or maybe living with Ben spurred a realization that there were two halves to me. Maybe I was more than just a product of my mother. Maybe my other half was much better than the half I knew.

"Do I look like him?" I asked.

I felt like I looked different than everyone in my family.

"No," she scoffed. "You look like my side of the family. You look nothing like him, and he wanted nothing to do with you. He told me to abort you, and you're lucky I didn't."

Still, I daydreamed that my dad would walk into my classroom and search through the faces sitting behind the wooden desks. Somehow, he would recognize me immediately. I imagined that he had known nothing about me, but as soon as he learned about me, he just had to find me and rescue me because he knew how toxic Mom was.

He would walk straight toward me, the entire room watching this tall, handsome man, a stranger who looked so familiar, walking to the ugly, unwanted girl who sat at the very back of the class so she didn't hear the whispers and laughing of the other kids. And he would walk right up to my desk and look at me with the saddest yet most determined eyes I had ever seen. He'd stand there looking at me, with his strong shoulders softening, his face filling up with emotions, and his blue eyes filling with tears.

"Come with me," he would say. "I didn't know about you, and I am so sorry. It's me, your dad. You are mine, and I will protect you now and forever. I love you, Kimberly, and I can't take back what has happened to you, but I promise I will never let anyone hurt you again."

These daydreams got me through the long hours in class. I had a hard time concentrating, and my mind would continuously wander. My schoolwork was easy, except for algebra. I could see the answer but had trouble with the steps to show my work. And for me, math was about fact-based results, which was not how my life was. I had way too many variables, what-ifs, and contingency plans just to survive. Even though I was still only 12, I was on my own, always thinking about what the worst thing that could happen was and how I'd survive it. I drew my strength believing that I was not like my mother and that unlike her, I knew what love was. I knew how to love and have compassion. I also knew the face of hate, which scared me, and I never wanted anyone to have to live the way I did, with no security, belonging, or peace. I loved when Gram or my aunts would call. They didn't call much, but when they did, it was like safety was at the other end of the phone. Hearing their voices made me happy but homesick. I knew I couldn't say why I didn't want to be with Mom.

She made a point of staying close when I was talking to them, so I would just say how much I missed them and that I didn't like Kansas. Every time, my aunts just assured me that I needed to give it time and I would like it eventually. My heart sank when I heard them trying to convince me that I was where I should be. I wondered if they really believed that, if they knew how awful she was to me, or if maybe, just maybe, they knew exactly who and what she was, and life was just easier for them with her gone. I wanted to scream, to tell them everything she did to me, to beg to come home. Instead, I remained silent. I figured, in their minds, I was just a homesick kid who hadn't adjusted to her new surroundings.

The only one who didn't dismiss my pleas to come home was Gram. Nevertheless, her reply was always the same: silence for a few seconds followed by a throaty "She is your mother, she wants you there, and I am not your mother, so you have to stay." After the first few calls, I stopped asking. Their calls became less frequent over the next few months, and when they did call, I pretended that I had homework or went outside to avoid being put on the spot when asked if I wanted to say hi. Even though I missed hearing their voices — especially Gram's — the rejection was more than I could bear.

Chapter 17

My mother never looked for a job in Kansas. She lived off the system. She received a Social Security check and a VA check that arrived on the 3rd of each month, unless it was a Sunday or a holiday. She received these checks because Ritchie had died and left us behind. She refused to buy me clothes or shoes, saying that she barely had enough to pay bills. She was 31 and usually stayed up all night doing things and going places I didn't want to know about. I pretended not to hear the car leaving late at night or notice what time she went to bed.

I was able to land a job next door babysitting and cleaning the house. The mom, Becky, was a registered nurse, and her husband was a cop. She said she would pay me 50 cents an hour to watch her three kids, aged one, two, and four, from 4 to 8 p.m. I had to cook and feed the kids dinner, clean the living room, bathroom, and kitchen, bathe them, and have them in bed before she came home. She often forgot to pay me and had the nerve to make me remind her that she owed me money. So much of the time, I didn't get paid at all because I didn't have the nerve to stand up for myself. And when I did get paid, it was for less than I had earned, but I never called attention to that because I was grateful for getting anything even though I worked hard.

Carl, the husband, worked second shift, so I rarely saw him and dealt only with her. I always found her a little strange, but I couldn't put my finger on what was off. Her house smelled like a skunk, and after work, she always listened to Deep Purple, burned incense, and hung out with a boy named Brad. He was the 18-year-old who lived down the block. He had long hair, pulled back into a low ponytail, and wore tight jeans and t-shirts with no sleeves. Carl was the complete opposite of Brad, from what I could see. He had short hair and a nondescript face, and he never said anything to me when he was outside doing yard work on his days off. He didn't even look at me or acknowledge my existence. At the time, I figured he saw something wrong with me, so I never spoke to him.

Despite the dismal and often nonexistent pay, this job allowed me to buy myself clothes, shoes, and sanitary pads — none of which Mom ever paid for. She only bought things for David. Mom signed us up for government cheese, canned meat, powdered milk, and anything else she could score for free. Several times, I searched the clearance racks at K-Mart, trying to find something that was pretty and that I could afford. Most often, I would pull the tags off and stuff them in a pocket of jeans or a sweater on a nearby rack, taking the clothes to a salesperson to ask the price, hoping it would be less than the tag had stated. Sometimes this worked, and sometimes it didn't. I knew that it was wrong to rip the tags off, but I felt justified because I just wanted to be like the other kids, and after all, I wasn't stealing. I was just hoping there was a chance I could buy something that would let me fit in.

As far as sanitary pads, if I didn't have money to buy them (which was often), I would use paper towels. When I was in school, I used toilet paper because there weren't paper towels in the restrooms. It's not like any of these actions made me popular. I was just trying to stick out somewhat less than I already did.

Living with Mom and David was even worse than I had imagined. I knew she would be mean — even vicious — toward me. And I expected her to let David do whatever he wanted, including breaking, stealing, and pilfering through my things. I expected her to beat me, burn me with cigarettes, humiliate me, and make me feel worthless. What I hadn't counted on, however, was sloth, benign neglect, and her complete dependence on me to run the household.

Every day, she slept until I came home from school and then spent the afternoon and early evening sitting on the porch, smoking in a filthy muumuu. She wore it for days, showering maybe once a week, which meant she always smelled like smoke and urine. She was overweight and hardly ever took showers. Most of the time, she took what she called a "PTA bath." This meant she used a wet washcloth and cleaned her "pussy, tits, and ass." This never got her really clean, and she always stank.

I bought the groceries with the money I earned. All she would buy was cheap junk food. I did all the cooking and cleaning, and I worked, earning the only income in our house, aside from the government checks we received in the mail. If I didn't work, I don't know how we would have survived this period of my childhood.

This side of my mother was new to me. Even though Gram would yell at her about not helping out when we were all under one roof, I didn't realize that she would be — that anyone could be — as negligent about their home, their children, or even themselves as my mother was during this time. When we lived with Ritchie and later with Ben, she cooked, did laundry, and took showers, but without a man to impress, she did none of those things.

The abuse wasn't quite what I expected, either. This period was similar to the one after Ritchie died, but now it seemed worse because I was older, and I had had a small taste of normalcy after living with Gram. Now I knew what normal was supposed to look like, and there was nothing normal about my situation. If I did something wrong, Mom told me she was going to send me to a home for unwanted girls. The beatings started again, but they were no longer with the belt across my bare bottom. Now, they were hard hits across my face with the back of her hand. The cigarette burns continued, but now she burned the top of my head. I wasn't sure if this was to hide them or to catch me off-guard as she walked up from behind me.

I had never felt more afraid or more uncertain in my life. I never knew what she would do next. One morning, I woke up for school, went into the bathroom, and found a baggie of blue, oval pills on the floor. I had seen these same pills on one of the overhead projector slides in a school assembly on drugs. Fear rushed through my body. In the assembly, the speaker told us that drugs were evil and that they would ruin our lives. They'd make people turn into abusive addicts. And now they were on my bathroom floor.

Oh my god, I thought. *She is using drugs, and she is going to get worse, and I am going to get beat more.* They told us that if we saw drugs, we should tell someone — a parent, teacher, pastor, or the school counselor. That we shouldn't be afraid to tell because they would protect us, and it was the right thing to do.

As soon as I arrived at school that morning, I went to the counselor's office. She wasn't there yet, so I sat in front of her office, anxiously waiting to tell her that my mother had drugs in our house, hoping she would call Gram, so I could go back with her.

The counselor, a heavy-set, middle-aged woman whose skirt and perm were both too tight, arrived after the first-class bell had rung. She was carrying a large bag of files, and when she saw me, she seemed more annoyed than welcoming.

"Shouldn't you be in class?" she asked, as she reached into the large bag, fishing for office door keys.

"I need to report that I saw drugs. The assembly said we were supposed to tell someone," I said, sheepishly.

She opened her door, walked in, switched the lights on, and dropped her overstuffed bag behind her desk.

"Come in and take a seat," she said.

As I sat down, she took out a black notebook from the front drawer of her desk.

"What's your name?" she asked.

"Kim," I said.

"What grade are you in?" she asked.

"Seventh," I said.

"What students did you see using drugs? And where were they smoking them?" she asked.

I sat there for a minute, not understanding her question. Immediately, I was scared to tell her what I had seen. She thought I was ratting out another student for smoking pot, which I had seen kids do. I'd also seen Becky smoke pot while she fooled around with the neighbor boy. None of that seemed scary. To me, it was like smoking cigarettes, which my mom did all the time. These blue oval pills on the bathroom floor, on the other hand, were another story. They scared me because I thought they were what drove my mother's rage, and I had to make that stop. I was tired of being afraid and just wanted to go back home to Gram's. I was hoping with everything I had that being brave enough to tell would make that happen. And so I did.

I took a deep, trusting breath because, during the assembly, the tall man at the podium said if we came forward, we would be safe and protected.

"It's not a student," I said. "It's my mother. I found blue pills on the bathroom floor in a baggie. And..." I paused. "She is mean and hits me a lot."

I wasn't brave enough to tell the whole story. The counselor looked up for a brief moment looking less excited than she had looked minutes before. After a brief pause, she continued to take notes. I took a leap of faith and told her what I thought she needed to hear.

"I'm afraid that my mom might be using drugs." I left out the extent of her beatings and rage, hoping that the evidence I found would be enough.

She didn't look up as I told her about the baggie of pills. I went on to say that she acted really weird and slept a lot. I was trying to convey to her that my mom was using drugs, hoping it would be enough for her to let me not go home. I even prayed that the counselor would be so appalled and worried for my safety that she would call the police, and they would come to take her away. Then they would have no choice but to send me back to Gram's. Telling the truth about why I was so scared of my mother was very hard because I didn't want to tell all the real things that made me scared of her. The mood swings were now worse, the horrible things she said to me were now worse — if that was even possible — and the rage in her eyes was now smoldering, and she would look at me like a snake ready to strike at any time. So I didn't say any of that. I stuck to the bare minimum of facts and waited for her to finish writing. I sat there feeling very naked and exposed.

"You know, you can tell me the truth," She said. "You're safe."

"I am telling you the truth. I saw blue pills on the bathroom floor. I think they're my mom's," I said. She knew I was holding back and asked questions to make me feel safe, but I didn't. I really thought she believed me until she took a long deep breath and said, "You can tell me the names of the students you saw. What drugs were they doing?"

"It wasn't students!" I repeated. "It was my mom who was doing the drugs," I replied.

She let out a disappointing sigh, laid down her pen, and said, "Thank you for reporting this. I will follow up."

What did I just do? I thought. *She doesn't care. She didn't even listen to what I said. If she had, she would look at me. She would say something that would make me feel safe and protected.*

Instead, she picked up her pen, wrote me a pass for being late, and that was it.

"Well, that was all for nothing," I said to myself as I walked to my first-period class. I realized at that moment that nothing was going to change. I blamed myself for being naïve enough to think anyone would help me. It was clear to me at that moment that no one cared, and I was on my own.

When I got home that afternoon, I expected to see my mother lying on the pullout bed of the couch in the living room, but she wasn't. She slept there because her room was so full of shit that you couldn't even make a pathway through it. It had piles of old newspapers, filthy clothes, and ashtrays overflowing on the floor. The carpet around it had burn marks from the hot ashes and butts that fell out. I thought it was strange that she wasn't there, but I didn't think much else of it until I walked toward my room and saw her standing in the hallway, fully awake, waiting for me to come home.

"I hear you went and spoke to the counselor today," she said. I felt as if her eyes were trying to bore a hole into me.

"No, why would I?" I lied. I tried to make my way around her toward my room. My mind raced with fear, my body started to tremble. I wondered how she knew — how the counselor could tell her. The counselor had said I was safe, and I thought she meant she wouldn't tell my mother I had confided in her.

Her rage arrived in full force. "The counselor called me today saying you came to her because you thought I had drugs in the house," Mom was screaming now. She had followed me into my room and was now hovering over me as I sat on my bed.

"Did you tell her there were drugs here?" she screamed.

"No," I replied, hoping she would back away and believe me.

"Don't you fucking lie to me!!" she wailed. She took her hand and hit my face so hard I nearly blacked out. She stormed out of my room, leaving me lying on my bed sobbing. I felt so stupid for thinking that telling someone would make any difference. My mother's voice rang in my head, reminding me that I was a mistake, one that should have been aborted with a coat hanger.

Chapter 18

The last few months of that school year were pretty much a repeat of the day before. I hated living in that house, which was filthy no matter how much I cleaned it. Cockroaches had now moved in and taken over. Instead of curtains, there were sheets nailed across the windows. I still had no friends and didn't sleep much because my brother was in the same room, and I knew if I fell asleep, he would steal my things — or break them. Gram would call sometimes but not very often, and I wasn't allowed to make long-distance toll calls.

It was during these months that I started listening to music to escape. I saved enough money to buy a small clock radio at K-Mart. I lay on my bed when my brother was outside and listened to what was playing on the radio. I listened to all types of music — pop, country, jazz, and classic rock. I would spin the knob and roll through the stations until I found something that made me want to stop and hear more.

That little $9 clock radio was my only friend. I unplugged it before I went to school and hid it under my bed in an old shoe box. Then every day, once I was home from school and had finished all my chores and cleaned for Becky and the coast was clear, I would bring it out and listen to it as I did my homework until it was time for bed.

On the last day of school, I overslept. A thunderstorm had knocked the power out. My mother came into our room screaming, "Get your ass up and on the bus, or you'll have to walk."

Startled, I jumped up, got dressed, and forgot to hide my radio. It was on the floor next to my bed. That day was the last day of seventh grade, and I was looking forward to it because it was a half day, and there was no classwork. I didn't need to say goodbyes or sign people's memory books like most kids did. For one thing, I didn't own a memory book, and for another, I knew that if I did, the pages would be empty because no one would want to sign it.

When I opened the front door, I expected to see what I normally saw — my mother still lying on the pullout sofa bed. So when I saw that she was in the kitchen, I was totally surprised. She was making tuna salad (again, totally surprised) until I saw my brother sitting at the table waiting to be fed.

"Why are you home?" I asked, knowing that she probably didn't make him go to school. This happened frequently. She would not get him up and ready, and just not make him go. She always had different sets of rules for the two of us. I walked into my room, shut the door, and quickly dropped to my knees and reached deep under the bed for the shoe box. I slid it out and noticed how light it felt as I pulled it toward me. And then it hit me. Fear rushed over me, like the fear I had felt when I saw Holly laying on the floor. I quickly stood up and looked at the floor next to my bed where I had left the clock that morning. It was right where I had left it. A rush of relief came over me. Thank God.

I sat on my bed and reached down to turn the radio on. I guess seeing it in one piece made me overlook the fact that the time wasn't showing on the front of the clock. I turned the knob to turn the radio on. Nothing happened. Hmm. Maybe I unplugged it before I went to bed last night. The outlet under my bed was about a foot back. Again kneeling on my knees, I reached, feeling the floor for the cord to plug it back in. My hand found the cord and followed it to the end for the plug. As my hand worked its way to the end of the cord where the plug should be, I felt the end with no plug. Panicking, I pulled the cord to see what had happened, and it was like finding Holly all over again. I began to sob. The cord had been cut, and the plug was gone.

No more music. No more closing my eyes so I could pretend I was in a place the song talked about. My brother walked into our room and started laughing at me, as I sat on the floor with the cut cord in my hand. And at that moment, my heartache turned to anger, which made me want to fight back, to stand up for myself. Some atrocities made me forget I was in survival mode, and that never ended well.

I stood up and pushed him onto his bed. This was the first time I ever did anything like this to him, and he looked surprised. I didn't hurt him at all, but he came back at me with the same stone-set rage expression on his face that Mom had when she would come at me. He recoiled quickly from his bed and punched me in the face. He may have been four years younger than I, but he was much stronger. I could feel his hatred in his punch, and his brutality echoed our mother's. He knew I wasn't strong. He had watched my mother beat me down both physically and verbally his whole life, so when I shoved him, he knew that it was a knee-jerk reaction, and his retaliation was to make me pay for even thinking of standing up for myself or for trying to make him pay for what he did to my radio.

The punch hurt, but I thought that we were even and that he wouldn't tell on me. But after he punched me, he started crying, howling at the top of his lungs. I sat there, face throbbing, thinking maybe somehow he hurt himself when he hit me, and I felt bad. I felt bad. I always blamed myself when something went wrong, even when I was the victim. I wasn't smart enough to see his plan. At eight years old, he knew exactly how to manipulate the situation in his favor, and it played out exactly the way he wanted.

She came into the room after hearing his screams and shouted, "What the fuck is going on?!"

"Kim punched me," he sobbed. "She hit me for no reason and pushed me so hard I hit my head on the wall."

I stood there in disbelief but had no voice to tell the truth. I was outnumbered, and I knew it.

"Why did you hit him and push him?" she screamed.

I knew it wouldn't matter what I said, so I said nothing. I didn't get the belt that night because there wasn't one handy. Instead, she grabbed my hair on top of my head and looked me straight in the eye, and said, "I will send you to a home where unwanted girls go. Don't touch your brother again, or I will make you go."

She picked me up from my scalp and threw me toward my bed, my head hitting the wall.

The next day, Gram called. I was sitting in my dark room feeling hopeless and lost, with nowhere to turn and no one to talk to. The phone rang, and I heard my mother speaking, and her replies and mannerisms told me it was Gram — my last chance of escaping from this hell I was living in. On this day, I didn't pretend to be playing outside or too busy to talk. On this day, I took a leap of faith. I waited for my mother's conversation to wind down. It was always the same conversation.

"Have you found a job?" Gram would ask.

"No, I've been looking, but there's nothing available," Mom would lie.

How's the weather? How are the kids? I knew the questions because I heard her replies and lies. When the time came, I got off my bed and opened my bedroom door, pretending not to notice her on the phone. I walked toward the kitchen for a glass of water. My mother didn't like talking to Gram, so when she saw me, she immediately handed the phone over and said in the receiver, "Here. Talk to Kim."

I knew she would do this and had planned my next moves in my dark room, head still pounding from the day before. The beginning of our conversation was normal. How was school? Are you making any friends? The usual. I asked about how my aunts and cousins were, and how my uncle was as well. Finally, she asked me how my brother was, and I could no longer pretend everything was okay. By this time, my mother had stepped outside to sit on the front porch to have a cigarette, and I had moved all the way back to the back of the kitchen, where the door to the garage was. Although I had planned this conversation, and in my plan, I was calm and concise as I told Gram what was happening, real life was quite different. I started to cry, stumbling over my words while telling her that he would hit me, steal from me, and break my things on purpose. That I had to share a room with him and didn't feel safe, that he would come in when I was changing or walk into the bathroom when I was taking a shower all the time. I couldn't keep it in anymore, and the words couldn't come fast enough. I sat on the peeling, dirty linoleum floor next to an overflowing trash can and begged her to let me come back home.

"Please, Gram, please!" I said over and over again. Not once did I tell her about the abuse I received from my mother, which was a hundred times worse. I was too afraid to tell the whole story because I knew that she would have to confront my mother from 1,400 miles away. And then I would be left again with no one to protect me. But I thought if I told on my brother and begged her not to say anything, I was safer. I'm not sure why — maybe because I knew that Gram knew what kind of child he was, having to deal with him herself.

Gram didn't ask questions during or after. She was silent throughout the entire conversation, and when I finished, there was an uncomfortable silence that made me feel exposed, naked, and vulnerable. *Oh, my god,* I thought to myself. *What did I just do?* Panicking in the silence, I quickly interjected and said, "I'm sorry, Gram. Never mind what I said, I'm just tired. I have to go now. I'm sorry."

I hung the phone up quickly, wanting to break the connection because the silence was too painful. I thought my leap of faith fell woefully, fatally short. I thought that if I told her the horrible things that were happening, she would say something, anything.

I cried myself to sleep that night, burying my face in the pillow, so my sobs were silenced. My mind raced, trying to figure out how I was going to get through this. What if she calls and tells my mother what I said? *Please, God, don't let her. Please...* Those were my prayers as I fell asleep that night.

The next night, around the same time, the phone rang, and I answered it.

"Hello," I said. The voice on the other end of the line scared me. It was Gram.

"Hi Kim," she replied.

My heart started to race. I was afraid she was calling to tell my mom what I had said.

"Mom's not here," I lied. She was outside smoking, like normal.

"That's okay," she said. "I called to talk to you."

Immediately I apologized for what I had said the night before and tried to backpedal.

"What he does isn't a big deal," I said. "I shouldn't have tattled, Gram. I'm sorry." *Please don't tell her!* My mind was screaming.

"I have bought a one-way ticket for you to come home. I will tell your mother it's just for the summer. We will deal with the details later," she said.

This time, the silence was on my end of the phone. Sitting in the same filthy place I did the night before, I saw a light at the end of the tunnel.

"Kim, are you there?" she asked.

"Yes," I replied quietly. "What if she won't let me come? I asked, thinking this was too good to be true.

"Don't worry about that," she replied, "I will make sure she will."

Again, silence on my part. My hands shook as I tried to process what was being said to me. And then she said, "I love you, Kim."

"I love you, too, Gram," I replied quietly. And she hung up.

Chapter 19

The next day, I waited for my mother to say something about my going to Connecticut, but it never came up. Every day for a week I waited, becoming more disheartened as the days went by. Maybe she told Gram no. Maybe Gram changed her mind. But exactly one week after my conversation with her, the phone rang. I heard my mother talking, and I knew right away it was Gram telling her about the trip.

"How would she get there?" Mom asked. "I have no money to buy her a ticket just so she can have a vacation for the summer," she growled. A long pause. She wrote something down on a piece of paper that was on the table. Then she hung up the phone and went outside to have a cigarette. I went into the kitchen to see what she had written. " AMTRAK" with a date and time. The date was two weeks away. In 14 days, I'd be safe. I was going home.

The next day Mom told me about the trip. She said Gram needed me to help her at the house with the garden and that she had bought a train ticket for me to stay for six weeks. I had been figuring out how I would get out of making the return trip. I wasn't surprised that Mom was letting me go. She hated me being around. She found ways every day to remind me how I ruined her life. Her teeth fell out when she was pregnant with me. I stole all her calcium, and she told me this every time she took out her false teeth, yelling, "See what you did to me!?" She only kept me around so I could clean up after her — and for the Social Security check. She'd lose half of her Social Security and welfare checks without me living with her, but I didn't care.

Days before my trip, I packed my favorite clothes, which weren't many. I had worked hard for them, and they made me feel pretty when I wore them. The morning of my trip, I was ready to go by 5 a.m. We drove to the train station, my brother in front with her, and I in the backseat. This was the normal seating arrangement if we all went out. I still got car sick, but that didn't matter. I knew the train was all Gram could afford, and I don't blame her for thinking it was okay to send a 12-year-old girl alone on a train from Kansas to Connecticut. She was on her own when she was 12, leaving home to work as a nanny, so she could send her family money for food. I wasn't afraid, though. No stranger could be as dangerous to me as my mom, and I gave the possibility of anything happening almost no thought. In two days I would be home for good, and that was all I could think about.

The train ride was mostly safe and uneventful. We stopped in Chicago, and I got lost in the train station trying to find the bathroom and then again on my way back, trying to find my train. Both times I was helped by a stranger who asked where my parents were. I lied, saying they stayed on the train with my baby brother. I was just happy they believed me and that I made it safely to the restroom without peeing my pants and back to the train for the last leg of my journey. Having to think a few steps ahead was exhausting, and I was looking forward to being home at Gram's, where I could relax and let my guard down.

I was tired and a little motion sick when we pulled into my stop. I hadn't slept much because I was afraid I'd miss it. I saw Gram and Uncle Bobby waiting for me as soon as I stepped off the train. She looked the same, wearing a blue floral dress with a necklace made from some sort of dried seeds. She clutched her purse in front of her chest; her red nail polish was chipped from the work she had to do around the house. Uncle Bobby stood beside her; he hadn't changed either. He wore a stained blue polo shirt and jeans. He was a heavy-set man but looked like a kid younger than me. His hair wasn't combed, and taking showers wasn't something he did often. But he had a gentle soul and a huge heart.

"Hi Kim," he said. "Where did you go?"

"I went on a trip, but now I'm back," I said. I was too tired to explain what I thought he should already know. I didn't understand why Gram hadn't filled him in.

"How was your trip?" Gram asked as she reached out and pushed my bangs away from my eyes.

Gram had a thing about bangs hanging too low, and when I was younger, I hid in the bathroom from her many times when she threatened to cut them. I didn't mind haircuts, but when she cut my bangs, they were always crooked and made me look worse than I already thought I did.

But this time, when she reached out to push my hair to the side of my face, I saw her hand with the beautiful red ruby ring she always wore, and instead of dodging her, I stood there feeling safe. Her hand pushed the hair out of my eyes and brushed across my forehead, washing a wave of peace and safety over me.

These hands wanted me to be able to see clearly and cared about me. I felt that, standing in front of the train that brought me home. I had never been afraid of this hand, and on this day, I welcomed it, yearning for her touch. It was the first time in months anyone had touched me that wasn't to inflict harm — let alone in a gesture of love. The first touch that wouldn't leave a bruise or a scratch or permanent scar on my skin or my soul.

I am home, I thought, with a sigh of relief.

Chapter 20

The next few weeks were great. My cousins and aunts came to visit. We went to the community pool and to our favorite ice cream parlor. I played kickball with the kids in the neighborhood. I even learned that babies came out of a vagina and not out of your belly button, thanks to my younger cousin, along with the other facts of life. The things she told me were so weird and alien to me. And all I could think of was how could a penis, which I knew from pictures of Roman statues, even get into a vagina?

They seemed kind of limp and small, and they just hung there. The thought kind of grossed me out. But this knowledge also made me feel like a grown-up, and it seemed like such a big deal to my cousin that I pretended it was for me, too. I was more interested in playing kickball with the kids that lived on our street and making forts from the large tree by Gram's house.

One night, my cousin Kelly and I were listening to the radio in Gram's basement. Cheap Trick's "I want you to want me" came on. "I love this song!" I said.

"Me, too!" she replied. "I will miss you when you go back home. This has been a fun summer."

"I'm not going back," I said. "I'm staying here." I said it in a matter-of-fact way, thinking she would totally understand and be happy for both of us. But she wasn't happy at all. She was the polar opposite. Of course, she was. She thought I was creating issues again. Instead of begging to stay the night, now it seemed that I was scheming to not go back to where I was supposed to be. She didn't reply to my declaration.

Instead, she told her mother, Aunt Sandy, who called my mother. I don't know what was said, but Mom called the next day. It was the first

I'd heard from her since I boarded the train in Newton, Kansas. She hadn't called to make sure I'd arrived safely, but she did when she heard that I wasn't coming back.

I had told my aunt Sandy how I had to share a room with my brother and how horrible it was. I told her I didn't feel safe, being watched when I changed. How he stole my stuff and broke my things on purpose. She must have relayed this all to Mom because Mom started making promises.

"Come home," Mom said. "I will turn the garage into a room for you. It will be all new, and you won't have to share anymore."

I didn't say anything. I didn't believe her. Finally, she barked, "Say something, Kim!" frustrated by my silence.

"I'm staying here," I said and hung up the phone. Later that night, Aunt Sandy came into my room and sat at the edge of my bed.

"I know it's hard having to share a room with your brother, but your mom is going to make you a new room, and you will have your privacy back," she said. "She is trying, and you need to try too. You need to go back, Kim. You don't belong here." And then she got up and left the room.

I sat there feeling betrayed but not sure by whom. I couldn't tell her what really happened at Mom's. I stayed silent, too afraid and embarrassed to tell her all of the other reasons I didn't want to go. She was only doing what anyone would when trying to deal with a spat between a mother and her daughter. I knew I had done this to myself because I didn't speak up. Fear had taken my voice away and replaced it with silence. My mind, on the other hand, was not silent. It screamed, begged, and scolded me for being a coward — making me hate myself that much more.

The next morning, Gram was in the front yard pulling weeds, and I went out to help her. Mostly, I wanted to tell her that I didn't want to go back, hoping somehow she would say I didn't have to go. She

116

glanced up to see me come outside and continued pulling weeds. She didn't look up when I got close. It was like she was ignoring me or avoiding the conversation I wanted to have.

Finally, I said, "I guess I have to go back, huh?"

She stood up suddenly, looked at me with a hard face, and said, "She is your mother. I am not. That's where you belong."

And with that, she walked off past me without another word. No cigarette burns or beatings had hurt as much as her words did that day. It was clear my aunt and my grandmother didn't want me to stay. Gram broke my heart that day. She saw how my mother was to me. She had witnessed it herself and taken a blow to the jaw. But still, she was sending me back. Maybe Aunt Sandy just thought she was doing the right thing. She never saw the rage or felt the pain of being hit so hard that everything went black as you fell to the floor. But she did see how I lived in filth and how I was dumped at Gram's and ignored by Mom. That day, I was an unwanted problem with lots of baggage that no one wanted to let into their life. The burden of my existence was palpable. I packed my bag that night, so I could go back to "where I belonged."

Chapter 21

When I returned to Kansas, nothing had changed like she had promised. The house was still filthy, ridden with cockroaches, and stunk of garbage and smoke. There was no room built for me in the garage like she promised. The drive to the house from the train station was silent. I stared out the car window, knowing what I was coming home to. To welcome me home, Mom said, "Clean the kitchen before you even think of going to bed."

It was 9 p.m. when we got back, midnight in Connecticut. But I did as I was told. Dishes done, floor scrubbed, and trash out two hours later as she and my brother sat and watched TV in the other room. That night, I realized that this was my life. I started trying to figure out how to survive it. I knew she expected me to be her maid and whipping boy when she was pissed at whatever life dealt her. She was too lazy, too weak, and always blamed me for her shitty life situation. The shifting of blame buzzed in her mind like bees getting louder and louder in their nest. She didn't have the coping skills to deal with it.

I could handle being the maid, I decided; it was the unknown lashing out when these "bees" were set off that I couldn't handle. I never knew what I was walking into when I came home from school or when she woke up. I was walking on eggshells, constantly playing defense.

The next three years were pretty much the same. I would do what I was told, always had my chores and homework done way before she asked or checked. Despite being a "stupid, ugly, fat, mistake child," I was expected to earn straight A's on my report card. One time, I tried to change a B to an A on algebra to avoid a beating. I ended up getting twice the beating for "being shitty and not knowing why x didn't equal z." She still pulled my pants and panties down for these beatings. I was 13, embarrassed by how I had developed, and felt exposed and self-conscious. She knew it, too. She could see how I was different when she told me to take down my pants and panties. It was like this new hesitation from me was more of a challenge for her. "Do it," she'd say, "or it will be twice as bad." She honored every threat she made, and the more I resisted, the worse it got.

By the time I was in the tenth grade, I was tired. Tired of my brother stealing from me, breaking everything I owned, and watching me as I dressed. Tired of my mother telling me daily that I was stupid and that she should send me to a home for unwanted girls. Tired of hearing over and over again of how she should have taken a coat hanger and got rid of the thing that had ruined her life.

I was invisible in high school. I kept to myself and watched the other kids in the halls with their friends. Some even had boyfriends or girlfriends. These kids held hands in the hall and passed notes during class. When they opened the notes, they smiled and blushed and quickly stuck them in the textbook. I really wanted to be like these normal kids, but I kept to myself because I knew what would happen if I trusted anyone to be my friend.

One day walking down the hall to second-hour science class, I noticed a tall boy, taller than me, which was a first since I was now six feet tall and towered over everyone. Kevin was cute with dark, wavy hair. He didn't seem to notice me. I saw him again when our choir had to practice with the school band for the upcoming homecoming dance. He was sheepish and shy — not cocky like most of the other guys. I would watch him standing with the big drum he played hanging around his neck, not talking to anyone, just staring at the band director with a blank stare.

Before practice one day, he struck up a conversation about how lame school dances were. At first, I thought he was talking to someone else, even turning to see if someone had been behind me after he spoke. Nope. He was talking to me! I was mesmerized. He was nice to me! We started to hang out after these practices, talking about his favorite video game and how he got another high score at the arcade, or how he was able to play a new song on his drum set. I didn't share anything about myself. I just listened to all of his accomplishments and told him how great I thought he was.

He would write me notes and give them to me as we passed each other in the hall. They were short and said things like "I like you so much," or they'd have a heart with our initials in the center. We talked on the phone and saw each other as often as we could.

He met Mom twice, briefly. He rode his bike over to my house on two occasions. Both times I had to push the roaches that were crawling up the wall behind the sofa out of view. And both times, I felt like he was uncomfortable sitting in my filthy, run-down house. His family was very proper and way better off than I was. To them, I was trash. I felt this the first time I met his mom when she picked him up after a football game. She dismissed me like I wasn't even there, not even looking at me when the car stopped.

Then, after a couple weeks, the notes stopped. When I called his house, his mom said he was busy and that he would call back, but he didn't. He avoided me at school as well. Finally, after several days of trying to reach him, I caught him in the hall.

"Hey, Kevin," I said. I motioned for him to step to the side and talk to me. To my great relief, he did.

"What's going on?" I asked. "Why are you avoiding me? Did I do something wrong? What did I do to make you mad at me?"

Without looking at my face, he said, "My ex and I made up. Sorry. I called and told your mom this morning before school so she would know." *Why would he tell her?* I thought. To this day, I have no idea why. Maybe it was like asking for your daughter's hand in reverse, or to clear one's conscience for not having real feelings, or maybe he was as afraid of her as I was. His declaration hit me hard. I knew he was embarrassed by me and where I came from, but I thought he truly liked me. Maybe he did but cowered under the pressure he felt from his family. It didn't really matter either way. I was heartbroken. This all happened during my last-period class.

When I got home, Mom was sitting at the kitchen table, waiting for me to arrive, coffee in one hand and cigarette in the other. I walked toward my room, trying to avoid her. I just wanted to lie on my bed and cry.

"I'm not surprised he broke up with you," her words stopped me in my tracks. "No one wants you, and you are stupid for thinking anyone would. You're a piece of shit."

It was like a pot in my head came to a boil, and the fluid ran over the sides because the heat and pressure were too much.

"I hate you!" I screamed. "I hate you! I wish you had taken that coat hanger to end my life because it would be better than having you as my mother."

I ran to the bathroom. It was the only door that had a lock, and I knew she'd be right behind me. But I wasn't quick enough. Just as I tried to close the door, she burst through and grabbed my arm. I tried to push free, but the bathroom was so small, I couldn't, and she gained power. Her hand came at me and hit me in the face so hard that I spun across the room and hit my head on the edge of the tub.

Fifteen hours later, I came to. I was unsure how I got to my room, but when I awoke, I was lying on my bedroom floor, and the sun shining made my head pound. It was morning and time to get ready for school. I tried to move, but when I did, the room started to spin, and I was overcome with nausea. This was unlike any motion sickness I'd ever had. It was a thousand times worse. But I had to go school, I needed to be safe, and I knew I wasn't if I stayed home.

Chapter 22

Somehow, I managed to get myself vertical and go to class that day. I didn't change my clothes, and I don't remember brushing my teeth or combing my hair. It took everything I had to climb the two steps on the bus, clutching the rails tightly so I wouldn't fall.

When I got there, I went straight to the nurse's office. I told her my head hurt, and I felt like I was going to vomit. She was an older woman on the heavy side, and she must have had a mint in her mouth because the smell of it was so strong that I felt the vomit climb halfway up my throat when she spoke to me.

She took my temperature, which was normal, and tried to call my mother a few times with no answer. While she did this, I lay on the dark green vinyl mattress and closed my eyes. The cot was cool, and closing my eyes helped stop the room from spinning. I stayed in the nurse's office for the entire school day. My mom never called the school back, which was a relief. I must have dozed off because I woke up startled when the nurse shook me and told me it was time to go home.

Getting on the bus to go home was as miraculous a feat as it was to get there. The trek from the nurse's office to the bus may as well have been a trip to the summit of Mt. Everest. Only my determination to not let it happen again kept me putting one foot in front of the other. All I wanted to do when I got home was lie down in bed. I'm not sure if Mom noticed how sick I was when I walked through the front door, but she wasted no time.

"He never liked you," she said. "He was only using you." She let out a sinister laugh and asked, "Who would want you anyway?"

I trudged past her and made it to my room unscathed. The pounding in my head increased, and the pain felt like nothing I had ever felt before. The room was spinning, the floor seemed more like an ocean, and I felt like I was going to vomit. As I lay in the dark, hot room, her words and the sound of my heart pounded in my head. I pulled myself out of bed and went into the bathroom.

I just needed something to stop the pain, to make it go away. I grabbed the bottle that said "Pain Reliever." I opened it, poured a handful of pills into my palm, turned the faucet on, and shoved them in my mouth. As I choked them down, I prayed that I wouldn't throw them up. And I prayed for the pain to stop. Back in my room, my head was spinning and throbbing at the same time. I lay down and listened to my heart still pounding in my ears. The bed was spinning. I closed my eyes to make the spinning stop, but all I could see was her laughing at me.

When I opened them, her hateful face was hovering over me. She was blurry, and her voice was muffled. "How much did you take?!" she yelled. I tried to reply, but my mouth wasn't moving, and no words were coming out. I felt like I was encased in wet cement. I couldn't keep my eyes open, and the room was still spinning.

The next time I opened my eyes, there was a nurse asking me questions. She said my name over and over.

"You need to keep your eyes open, Kim," she said. "I need you to drink this," she said and handed me a small cup of black water. "You need to drink all of it."

The taste was horrible but not as bad as the vomiting that came after. I started to vomit violently over and over until there was nothing left in my stomach. Then I started to dry heave, which was just as painful but without relief. The nurse stayed in the room the whole time, holding a gray plastic basin by my mouth and rubbing my back as I threw up. After the heaving stopped, she wiped my face with a wet cloth and put a cool cloth on my forehead. She left the room and turned off the light, closing the door behind her.

I didn't know how I got to the emergency room, and as I lay in the dark room, I tried to figure out what had happened. My mind felt heavy, but as I lay there, I could hear my mother's voice outside the room.

"She tried to kill herself because of a boy that broke up with her," Mom told someone.

The voice on the other side of the door replied, "Unfortunately, this happens often with teenagers. Once we are sure she is stable, she will be admitted into the psych unit for observation."

Psych unit?!? I'm not crazy, I thought to myself. I screamed silently that she was lying. I wanted to tell them everything. But not only was I afraid of what she would do to me if I did but — what if she was right? All the horrible things she said I was, what if they were true? The thought was too much to bear.

They transferred me from the ER the next morning to the teen/young adult psych wing. I felt better physically. The meds I received in the ER helped with the pain from the concussion. My head started to clear up. I could see and hear people properly now, and they made more sense. I actually liked being in the hospital. Everyone was so caring and nice. They checked on me and brought me warm blankets and pitchers of ice-cold water because my throat was so sore from all of the vomiting.

When I was moved to the psych unit, I was apprehensive because I had no idea what to expect. I thought "psych unit" meant crazy people, ranting and talking to themselves or to nonexistent people, but what I saw were normal people sitting on sofas, eating Snack Pack puddings. It seemed so weird to me that a psych unit was so much homier than my home.

The psych ward had structure, and for the first time since staying with Gram three years earlier, I felt safe. I attended group counseling sessions and listened to others share their stories about why they were there. Some stories were like mine, but most were about drug abuse. Some went into great detail about the drugs and how they got high at an early age with their parents. Others just sat silently like I did. Although I didn't really know or understand drugs, the other kids' underlying story ran parallel to mine. Absent or neglectful parents. Either their parents were abusive like mine, and drugs were their escape, or their parents were addicts and shared their addiction with their kids. It was a distorted and disgusting type of parenting and another type of abuse in itself.

As I sat and listened to their stories, some of which I didn't understand because I had been so sheltered while living with Gram, I felt sad for them. Like me, they spoke about feeling lost and abandoned, trying to get through life the best they could with no support. They felt like they didn't belong anywhere, just like me. They were lost in the system and knew that people pretty much expected them to be failures because that's where they came from. Status quo.

I didn't share anything in the group. I couldn't because I had no idea where to start and because I wasn't ready to be judged. Although being in the unit made me feel safe, the kids there didn't. They pounced on every new person's story, making comparisons and downplaying the other's experience to make theirs much more painful, more horrible, and more unfathomable. This allowed them to blame what they were doing on their circumstances, not themselves. I, on the other hand, blamed myself for all the things that happened to me.

The days were very regimented. Everyone had groups they were made to go to and counselors they were scheduled to see. I attended the group sessions but wasn't assigned a counselor for a few days. I saw everyone going to their scheduled counselor visit, and I actually felt left out. Even in this place, I just wanted to be like everyone else. Finally, a tech informed me that I had been assigned a counselor and was to meet with him later that day. Finally, I was like all the rest. Despite this relief,

I had no intention of sharing what was going on in my life. I was desperate to feel normal, even in a psych unit where no one was normal.

The counselor sat in a dark room that was lit by only a desk light. When I walked in, he had my chart open and was reading. He briefly looked up and introduced himself.

"I'm Brian. I have been assigned to your case. Please have a seat," he said. He was young. He had shaggy hair, dark-rimmed glasses, and a striped sweater with his name tag pinned on the left corner of his chest. As I walked toward the chair, I wondered what I was supposed to say and why I was here in the first place. He faced me the entire time and waited for me to sit before speaking again.

"So, tell me why you wanted to kill yourself. What happened to make you take the pills?"

I was a little taken aback and instantly felt the need to defend myself, which was something I had never really done. He made me feel like I was a failure, and that made me mad.

"I didn't want to kill myself," I snapped. "I took too many pills by accident because I fell and hit my head." This was the truth, albeit the Reader's Digest version. I waited for him to ask me how I hit my head, but he didn't. He didn't seem all that interested.

"The pain was so bad, and it wouldn't stop," I explained. "I just wanted to make the pain stop, not die."

He looked at me, read more of my chart, and finally said, "Well, I think this was accidental, and you don't belong here. The staff have said you have been very compliant, and we have had no other behavioral issues. I will have them call your mom, and you should be home by dinner tomorrow." He smiled and dismissed me. He turned back to his dimly lit desk and jotted down notes in my chart.

Great. Back to my hellish reality. Mom said nothing when she picked me up. She was silent the entire ride home, which was fine with me. I had my mind on other things, such as wondering who else knew what happened. I was sure no one knew the real story, only whatever story she told them. I was embarrassed because she told them I tried to kill myself, which wasn't the truth; I just wanted the pain to stop, the beatings, the humiliation, the feeling like I was a mistake and unwanted by anyone to stop.

I tried thinking of ways to explain my absence without telling the truth. So many scenarios ran through my head, and although the truth was the easiest to explain, it was not an option. To my relief (and disappointment), no one said anything. Not a word when I spoke to Gram or my aunts after I had returned home. I was in the hospital for almost two weeks and was sure they were told. Maybe I was hoping they would be concerned enough to ask, even though I was scared they wouldn't believe my made-up reasons.

I waited for them to say something when they called, but they never said a thing. And neither did I, thinking maybe Mom hadn't said anything. Maybe she was afraid that I would finally speak up, but then I realized that wasn't true either because she knew how afraid I was of her. She knew that she was the predator, and I was the scared, weak prey at her mercy. And when I got out of line, she bared her snarling teeth and often went in for the almost-kill to make me know where I stood.

Chapter 23

I shelved this entire incident in the back of my mind and forged on, pretending it never happened. She didn't say anything about it, and the beatings and cigarette burnings started to decline. The physical abuse was now replaced with verbal abuse and habitual groundings, more so than before. She spent the rest of my high school years calling me fat and ugly — and stupid because I didn't get straight A's on my report cards. She grounded me for one month for every minute I came home late. She calculated the time it should take me to come home from the grocery store, where I had gotten a part-time job.

I was dependent on rides from coworkers. Work was ten miles from home, so walking wasn't an option. I would give them gas money, but I hated asking, and she wouldn't come to get me. Because I never made it home by her calculated time, I was always grounded. Those coworkers were my entire social life. And because of that, I worked as much as I could, offering to pick up shifts every chance I got. I spent most of the money I made paying people for rides, and some of the rest I spent on clothes at Kmart, trying unsuccessfully to look like the pretty girls. What little was left I had to hide because both Mom and David would steal it if I left it in my purse when I was asleep or in the shower. I knew she stole from me as much as my brother did. I watched her steal from Gram for years. Sure enough, when I had five dollars go missing, all of a sudden, she had money to buy cigarettes.

One night I was at work, and my ride home was sent home early. I called home to ask if she could pick me up. I was 17 by then.

"If you're old enough to have a job, you are old enough to figure out how to get your ass home...on time," she said. "You know what will happen if you are late."

As I hung up, Mark, a stock boy who was a few years older than I, came by. "Need a ride?" he asked.

I didn't really know him. He had worked there longer than I had and covered the cashiers when they went on break. Beyond him covering for me, I hadn't said two words to him. He was shorter than I was, with a stocky build and short, jet-black hair. His round face had a little acne and a scraggly mustache, but he had a nice smile and dark brown, kind eyes. He always wore a plaid shirt, jeans, and hiking books. He was always polite and friendly.

Sheepishly, I replied, "I can't pay you for it tonight, but I can on payday."

He half smiled at this. "Free of charge," he said.

Wow. I was grateful for the ride, surprised by his kindness, and instantly aware of his attention.

Mark drove a 1972 metallic-blue, short-bed Chevy truck. It was so pretty and so well taken care of. As I got in the car, I was surprised to find myself nervous and realized I didn't know his intentions. I sat as close to the passenger's side door as I could, gripping the handle, just in case. Thankfully, he didn't seem to notice my apprehension and popped in a cassette. Van Halen came blaring on the speakers, which only added to my anxiety. He seemed so confident and free, and every once in a while, would look at me out of the corner of his eye and smile. For the first time ever, I felt seen.

When we got to my house, he asked, "When do you work next?"

"Tomorrow at 3:00," I responded.

"Okay," he said. "I'll come by and pick you up."

Again, I felt surprised and relieved to not have to ask Mom for a ride. He kept offering me rides one at a time, and I finally told him how much it meant to me.

"I really appreciate you driving me," I said one day on our way home.

"Yeah, it's no problem.... How did you get to work before?" he asked.

"Sometimes my mom takes me, but a lot of the time, she won't, so I have to ask someone," I said. "My mom gets really mad at me if I'm late. For every minute I'm late, she grounds me for a month. She doesn't want me to be out."

"Well, I'll make sure you can get to work and home on time," he said.

And from that day on, he was my ride — even when he wasn't working.

One day at work, the customer service cashier, Crystal, approached me. She had big, dark-brown hair, heavy mascara, and looked like she was dressed for a Madonna music video.

"Say, I have to tell you," she started. "Ever since Mark started driving you, your mom calls to make sure you're actually here. She also asks what time you get off work."

I wasn't surprised, but I was so embarrassed. I didn't want people to know what I was living with. It was humiliating.

But it was also helpful because I knew what time my mom started the clock. So anytime I could get off work early, I would, so I could spend more time with Mark in his truck. Often on drives, he would tell me I was pretty, and we would talk about happy endings and fairytale relationships.

He also loved to talk about his truck and was constantly pimping it out. I was impressed with his truck, too, in part because it was so much better than Mom's Ford Galaxy, which smelled like urine because she had developed incontinence and was filthy from her lack of showering and cigarette smoke.

Mark didn't smoke, which was a relief to me. He first kissed me in his truck in front of my house after driving me home from work. There was silence between us, but he kept looking over at me and smiling.

His eyes were kind, and I felt the chemistry between us. At this moment, he leaned over and kissed me goodbye. Van Halen played on, and I felt special. I could tell by the way he looked at me at work that this moment would happen soon, but I didn't know when. I blushed and smiled. "Goodnight," I said. "I'll see you tomorrow." I was happy — all the way to my front door.

By the time I graduated high school, we'd been "dating" for three and a half months. Not that we ever actually went on a date. We never went to dinner or a movie or anywhere other than his truck. But we got to know each other in that truck, and I felt I could trust him. He told me he loved me and promised to take care of me and protect me. I believed his promises, and for the first time since Gram, I felt safe and loved. I told him I loved him, too. We didn't really talk much on these drives home, but the silence was safe, and the touch of his hands was reassuring. That was all I needed.

By this time, he had a pretty clear picture of my life with Mom. Sometimes, she would show up unannounced at work. My heart would sink as she pulled up in her car, waiting to take me home. She couldn't stand the idea of me finding any joy, and preventing Mark from driving me home took away my joy. If Mark was already working and couldn't drive me, she relished in my asking for a ride — and then demanded I pay for a full tank of gas.

Mark understood all of this. Shortly after I graduated, he said he wanted to spend the rest of his life with me.

"The day you turn 18, I'm going to come and get you, and we're going to grow old together."

It had never dawned on me that my future might be filled with love that would last forever. My eighteenth birthday was two months away, and I started counting down the days.

When I got home from school the next afternoon, Mom was sitting on the front porch in her nightgown, smoking a cigarette.

"I'm leaving," I said. I felt the strength growing in me. "And I'm going to have a good future. One day, I'm going to have a home and a career and someone who's going to come clean my house for me."

"No, you won't," she said. "You're going to be in the welfare line, just like me."

"I will never be like you," I said. And I meant it with every fiber of my being. "You are mean and hateful, and I would rather die than be like you!" I ran to my room and sat in front of the door, hoping and praying she wouldn't come knock it in like so many times before. Hours passed, and I slept in the same place I sat. The next day it was like nothing had ever been said – in fact, she ignored me. Not saying a word. Which was more than fine for me because I was dreaming of my freedom, which was only eight weeks away.

And so it was. On August 19th at 12:00 a.m., I was on the sofa, watching for him through the window. My duffle bag and purse were packed in my room. Mom was sitting at the kitchen table, smoking a cigarette and cutting coupons as I pretended to watch TV. Finally, his shiny blue Chevy truck pulled up. He beeped the horn, and I jumped off the sofa, grabbed my bag, and walked out the front door.

Mom followed me, screaming, "I will call the police!! You were born at 7:32 a.m. and are not legally 18 yet!"

Ha! I thought. *Tell that to the police.*

Mark opened the truck door for me, took my hand, and rescued me from my life.

Part 2

Chapter 24

We lived in Mark's apartment. I moved in in mid-August, and one month later, we were married. It was a whirlwind of escape and newness. He was always telling me how pretty I was. And he was so sweet and thoughtful in the things he said and little ways he found to delight me. He was full of promises — a life full of love, happiness, and a real family. And they seemed to be coming true.

The apartment was a small one-bedroom with a tiny kitchen and bathroom. But it smelled like fresh paint, and I loved it the minute I walked through the door. It was on the second floor, so it felt as if I were walking into a fancy hotel — and not at all like the dank shack I lived in with my mother. I didn't have anything to unpack except the small sack I had brought with me the night I left, but that didn't matter. The bright, freshly painted walls and freshly cleaned carpets of the apartment were like a blank canvas waiting for us to create our home.

I had not spoken with or seen my mother since Mark and his big, blue, steel steed of a truck came for my rescue. For the first time in my life, I felt free from her. Even when I'd lived with Gram, there was always the possibility of having to return to life with my mother. But that was gone now, and I felt truly liberated. Mark and I were enjoying the excitement of our whirlwind relationship, and I put her out of my mind. *She can't find me or hurt me now,* I said to myself whenever fears and doubts crept into my head. Mark and I slept as late as we wanted and did whatever we wanted.

I was finally in a place where bugs were not climbing on the walls or crawling in my blankets or in my shoes. And no one was hitting me. Everything was perfect, just like I had dreamed of. Every day before Mark came home, I would make sure the apartment was clean, and I always cooked his favorite meals. We even adopted a black cat and named him Ernie. We had our own little family, and I was doing everything I thought a wife should do because I didn't want to lose him.

One day, the phone rang. It was about the time Mark was about to get off work, so when I answered, I expected to hear his Kansas accent, but instead my hello was answered with, "You can't hide forever, Kim."

I slammed the phone down on the receiver, my heart racing as I started pacing the room. The phone rang again. Twenty rings and then a few minutes pause and then another round of ringing. "Just leave me alone!" I screamed at the tan push-button phone on the wall. It rang on and off for about thirty minutes, and by the time it had finally stopped, I was sitting in the corner of the living room floor with my legs crossed and my arms wrapped around me, rocking back and forth in the dark. *Why did she find me?* I kept asking myself over and over.

When Mark came home from work, I was sitting in the same spot on the floor. The room was now completely dark, and the fear of her finding me had made me incapable of doing anything. I didn't tell Mark the truth as to why I didn't want her to find me. He knew she was mean by the stories I had shared. But they were nowhere close to cracking the surface of abuse I had endured by her. And he was not intuitive enough to see anything deeper than that, so he just assumed I didn't want her to intrude on our new life.

Later that night, after I had put the calls in the back of my head, I went to Mark and asked him if we could have a code for him to call home. I told him that I didn't want to speak to her, and this way, I would know for sure it was him calling. This was several years before caller ID was available, let alone cell phones. He agreed to have a calling code and said when he called, he would let the phone ring twice, then call back. This way, I knew I could answer the phone. He never dug too deep as to why I needed this, and I didn't volunteer the ugly truth. The

135

code worked, and although the phone rang throughout the day, I would only answer when I was sure it was him calling.

The relationship continued to grow, and we spent much time discovering each other. He was always kissing and touching me, and though I enjoyed the attention, it was more for his enjoyment than mine. But I didn't care. I felt happy that I could make him happy in any way that I could and didn't think twice about it. I wasn't on birth control, and we were nowhere close to being careful. Shortly after we moved in together, my period was late. When I told Mark, he was not devastated, but not thrilled either.

"Well, I guess we have to get married," he said.

Most would be disappointed in a proposal like this, but I wasn't. The thought that he had to marry me — not that he wanted to marry me — lived in the back of my mind, as did the thought of me telling him I was late and that I may be pregnant was my way of trapping him so he wouldn't leave me. Maybe it was a little of both.

I had a happy life now, but I was constantly afraid that it would disappear. Although I had found happiness, I was still living in survival mode — always planning for the worst-case scenario and trying to be prepared. Deep down, I feared that one day Mark would be gone, in large part because my mother had instilled in my head that I wasn't worthy of love, and deep down, I thought he would figure this out, too. I just wanted a family. A husband who loved me forever. A man who I could trust and who would never leave. Deep down, I still felt not good enough, so I tried everything I could to be perfect.

We were married outside the courthouse, not a chapel. My wedding dress was a tan seersucker top and pants, not a beautiful wedding gown. Mark's father, mother, and brother were the only attendees. Not the fairytale wedding I had dreamed of, but I was okay with it because at least someone wanted to marry me. I couldn't quite shake the idea that maybe he was marrying me because he thought he had to, or worse, that I had trapped him into marriage by telling him I was late. But we were married nevertheless and about to start our lives together.

The day after we got married, my period came, and the doctor confirmed that I wasn't pregnant. I was heartbroken and worse, I felt like everyone thought I made up being pregnant so we would get married. I justified to them and myself that I must have miscarried, but everyone knew the truth and deep down inside, I did, too. One month later, I was pregnant, for real this time. I was so sick and missed so much work that I lost my job. Losing my job put a strain on our marriage. Money was tight as it was, and a baby on the way didn't help.

Once the vomiting subsided a bit, I got another job, this time at a local fast-food restaurant. The morning sickness was still there but not as bad, and my shifts were all from 5 to 10 p.m., so that helped. One night, I was working at the cash register, and I saw my brother walk in. My mother came in behind him, and they headed straight to where I was. I froze.

"I heard you are married now. And you are having a baby?" she said.

She stared at me as I stood on the other side of the counter, wishing I could run. My brother stood behind her, not saying a word but enjoying every moment of this, which was evident from the smirk plastered on his chubby face.

How did she know? How did she even know where I worked? She must have seen my perplexed expression as I stood silent, my mind racing. She finally broke the awkward silence and told me her neighbor had run into Mark at the grocery a couple days prior, and he had told her. He never mentioned this to me, and I was infuriated that he broke our promise to not speak to her, ever.

"I guess congratulations are in order," she said. "When is the baby due?"

Finally, I found my words. "Beginning of June," I said. "We're moving into a mobile home soon. Mark's parents, Earl and Marcy, cosigned the $5,000 loan for us. It's a 14x60 in the same trailer park as them." I don't know why I said all this. I guess I was trying to impress her, show her that I had my life together. I should have stopped, but I couldn't.

"We're having them for dinner in a few weeks. You should come." For the life of me, I don't know why I invited her. I was still very intimidated and afraid of her and wanted to protect my new life. But I also wanted her approval, to show her that I was just fine and had a life filled with love and a family on the way. That she was wrong about me.

"I'd love to," she said with an evil grin. Her stare was like a cat watching her prey squirm as it backed into a corner, fear-stricken and trying to figure out how it could escape while entertaining the villain at the same time. There were no warm fuzzy feelings or joyous hugs, no celebratory exchange that typically occurs after an announcement of the first grandchild coming. It was more like she saw that I was happy and was going to make sure it didn't last.

Just like that, I'd invited her to the one place I didn't want her — and she was coming. *Holy shit, what was I thinking?* My mind spun on how I could make this perfect. *I will show her,* I kept saying to myself.

The night arrived in no time. I made meatloaf, Mark's favorite. Not a five-star meal, but it was his favorite just the same. I made sure that it had a nice wide stripe of ketchup down the center, just the way he liked it. I worked most of the day cleaning the house and cooking. I tried to make sure everything was spick and span, knowing that she would judge everything. She arrived early, before Mark got home, and walked through the door without even knocking. This scared the hell out of me, seeing her in the doorway as I walked into the living room from the back of the house.

"Make me some coffee," she barked and lit a cigarette at the kitchen table.

It was like I was back at her house. I didn't ask her to not smoke in my house. I just obeyed her command and kept my mouth shut. Mark came in a few minutes later with his parents. His dad was carrying a bottle of Seagram's 7, and his mother, Marcy, was the oldest looking forty-two-year-old woman I had ever seen. Her hair was bright white and teased high into a French twist. Her skin was almost as pale white as her hair. She was uncomfortable sitting at the table because she kept fidgeting in the chair and looking at the clock.

My mother was unkempt as ever. She had no etiquette for proper greetings. Her conversation starter was "Pour me a nice tall glass, no ice, just booze," directed at me, Earl still owning the bottle that he sat in front of his place setting. After a few moments of pleasantries, they all took their seats around our small, modest dinner table. I served them all, not sitting to eat once. I was their waitress, and they talked about me like I wasn't even in the room.

After dinner, Mark's parents and my mother all went outside and smoked. They had been drinking 7 and 7s. I was the only one not drinking, and Mark retreated to our tiny living room to watch TV like he did every night. I finished the dishes and walked outside, where they were seated. The conversation immediately stopped. I felt like I had walked into a room where I shouldn't be. Marcy looked up at me, and her expression was hard. Earl immediately stood up and said "Let's go." And they left, neither of them saying another word.

I looked at my mother, wondering what she had done. She was still sitting in the same spot, smoking her cigarette, watching this all happen — and watching my reaction. I waited.

"I had to tell them, Kim. It's only fair," she said as she smashed her cigarette in the ashtray and lit another. "They are going to figure it out soon enough." Her evil eyes watched me, and the corners of her mouth curled up into an evil smile.

"Tell them what?" I asked. My heart was racing. What could she be talking about? Maybe she told them about how I wet the bed as a kid, or worse, how I had to go to a psych unit. My mind was searching for the worst thing I did that she could tell them.

"That the baby may not be Mark's."

At that moment, my mind stopped searching for all the imperfect things about myself, and I stood frozen in disbelief. Her words were like knives thrown at me. *Where did this even come from?* I thought. *Why would she even say this?* And at that moment, I was so mad at myself. Mostly because I was shocked that she had done this. I hated myself for allowing it to happen because I did. I thought I was safe from her, but I wasn't. And I was still afraid of her, so I said nothing. I just walked inside with tears rolling down my face, past Mark, who was passed out on the sofa, and into my room and locked the door. I lay there crying for a while and then put my hands on my belly and swore to my unborn baby that I would never, ever hurt it. I swore that I would be a good mommy and love and protect it forever.

As I made these promises to my swollen belly, I felt this little flutter, soft and faint like a butterfly, and at that moment, I felt a love so great it made my tears turn from anger, embarrassment, and fear to tears of joy and happiness. The lies told that night faded away when I felt my child move. This baby was real, and instantly, I loved it more than anything.

My in-laws, on the other hand, didn't forget what my mother said, and they carried doubts about whether Mark was the baby's father. It never came up in conversation, but I could tell Marcy didn't trust me. Every time I saw her, she asked when the baby was due and would circle back to asking when we started dating and who I had dated before him. She did this in a coy way, trying to be nonchalant, but I could see that she didn't trust me and didn't approve of me. At least she made somewhat of an effort to be civil when I was around, but Earl didn't

140

hide his doubts. He would make off-hand comments like, "I wonder who this kid's gonna look like." His yellowed mustache that curled over his lip failed to hide his suspicious grin when he said it. I could see why they would believe her. I mean, what mother would say something so horrible about her daughter?

Chapter 25

During my pregnancy, I did everything I thought the perfect mom-to-be and wife should do. I tried to please Mark, but I had no idea what that was. I focused on creating a nursery with a crib I found at a yard sale. I washed the used baby clothes that I also found at yard sales and tried to get all of the stains out of them, so they would look new for our baby.

I had no help from Mark, and he wasn't interested when I would show him the nursery or the clean stacks of cloth diapers that had been bleached over and over, so they were white again. And it became apparent that he really wasn't ready for the commitment of a family. He worked long hours at the grocery store, and when he came home, he sat in his chair and watched TV, eating the meal I had prepared for him. We didn't have much real conversation, and sex was pretty much obsolete because I was pregnant. He said that it would hurt the baby if he touched me. I felt so alone. The sweet conversations I had with my swelling belly became the only interaction I had with anyone.

The house was always clean, and the bills got paid one way or another. Sometimes I wrote a check that I knew would bounce; I just prayed that it would take a day or two to hit the bank. After everything I'd had to do to survive this far, floating a check was no big deal. I actually got pretty good at it. While he worked, I took care of everything at the house and marveled at my growing tummy. I felt this tiny creature squirm around. We didn't know the gender, but I felt (and hoped) it was a girl. I knew when she woke up and when she slept. I could feel her stretching and moving all the time. All these feelings were amazing because I knew she loved me, and I loved her.

Because I didn't have friends or a mother I could trust—and calling Gram was expensive because it was long-distance — I called the doctor's office with questions and concerns about the baby at least once a week. These phone calls made me very familiar with the nurses, and they all knew me and expected my calls. As time went on, I could tell they grew irritated with them, but I called anyway. I was alone and scared something was going to go wrong, and I didn't understand how my body was changing and what was normal and what wasn't.

During my 36-week appointment, the doctor finally gave me some information to help try to guide me during this pregnancy. He told me to start watching the baby's movements and pay attention to how many times I felt movements during the day. When I was 39 weeks, I noticed that her movements had slowed down, and she got much less active. When I called the doctor's office, the nurse told me to come in the next day.

We had to be there very early in the morning, and Mark had to work, so I drove myself. On the way there, I kept talking to my baby to see if my voice would make it move around. They did multiple tests and monitored the baby's heartbeat, which kept dipping. The doctor decided the best course of action was to get labor going and deliver this baby. They told me to come back to the hospital the next day and that there are all kinds of things a woman can do to induce labor, such as walk, drink castor oil, take hot showers with the water hitting the lower back...but that's not what the nurses told me to do when I got to the hospital.

Mark came this time. The baby coming must have become real to him, and we showed up at 5:30 a.m. as ordered. I was prepared for the methods they had described the day before, but instead, they put hot washcloths on my breasts and had me twist my nipples. I was so embarrassed and self-conscious. My sexuality at 18 was that of an adolescent who didn't know how to be sexually open. I didn't want

Mark to watch this, so I made him turn his head and face the other way. We did this for two days, but nothing happened.

The medical team decided to put me on Pitocin, a drug that causes contractions. What they don't tell you about Pitocin, though, is that it makes contractions stronger and more painful. After 48 hours, I was only dilated to four centimeters. Then, finally, my water broke, but the baby's heartbeat continued to dip during contractions. Once the water breaks, the clock really starts, and it's not good to be in labor much longer. So they decided to perform a C-section. I didn't know much about what that meant, but they explained it was major surgery, and I was scared. Mark wasn't really supportive, and I'm sure it was because he was 21 and was scared as well. But instead of being there, holding my hand and telling me it was going to be okay, he was on the phone with his parents, talking to them about the procedure and whatever else they spoke of. He finally came back right before they inserted the epidural.

I was given an epidural, so I could be awake during the delivery. I felt the pressure of the scalpel cutting me open, but there was no pain, at least. And at 11:49 p.m. on July 29th, 1985, Jessica Lynn entered the world. She was so mad that she had been taken from her special place. She was screaming and crying and covered in goo. And then I said her name. I had picked her name because I had once met a little girl with the same name while playing outside. She had beautiful long, red hair and the biggest eyes. She was a quiet little girl, and I imagined that she would be just like Holly Hobbie's sister if she had one.

"Don't cry, Jessica, Mommy's here," I said as the nurse brought her close to my face. As I spoke to her, she stopped crying and looked at me with the face of an angel. I looked into her big, dark eyes and felt something I had never felt before. It was an enormous love like I had this beautiful creation that loved me, and I was the only thing she needed. Her tiny lips were still quivering, and her eyes squinted because the room was so much brighter than she was used to, but I kissed her sweet forehead, and her breathing became calmer, and her tiny whines stopped. This feeling was like something one would only dream of, not one I had ever experienced but had seen on TV and wished for.

"Okay, Mom," the nurse said as she took my sweet Jessica from me. "We need to get this princess weighed."

I felt myself becoming very tired as they weighed her and checked her out to make sure she was okay, and I drifted off to sleep.

When I woke up a few hours later, the whole ordeal seemed like a dream. I was in a hospital room all by myself, and my baby was gone. I called the nurses' desk, and they told me that she had something called "wet lung" and had taken her to the nursery. I lost my shit. My fear that it had all been a dream suddenly morphed into fear that something was wrong with her. It was too much for my brain to process at once, especially in a sleepy, drugged-up state.

I sat in bed, crying, terrified that something was going to happen to my new baby girl — someone I needed so much. I already loved her with my whole heart and would give my life for her. And I was alone. I called Mark at home, but he didn't answer. Finally, after three hours, he came into my room, and I told him what was going on. He didn't say why he wasn't reachable or why he had left the hospital in the first place. My anger was extinguished because the nurse followed him into the room and brought Jessica to us, and suddenly, everything was better. I didn't ask him where he was. I was so preoccupied and didn't want to let go of this sweet little thing.

I had no idea how to take care of a new baby, but when we got home, I did my best. I was always worried that she would get sick, and I overreacted to every simple cough or sneeze. When she was two months old, she had a very bad virus. She was vomiting and had a high fever, and she needed to be hospitalized. They did a spinal tap to rule out meningitis. The whole ordeal was horrible. The meningitis test was negative, but she was diagnosed with Rotavirus and had to stay in the hospital for three days.

During that time, I started feeling sick, too, with ear pain, among other things. I wondered if I had what she had gotten. The doctor put me on antibiotics for an ear infection but failed to tell me that antibiotics can interfere with the birth control pill, which I was on. Eight weeks later, I was late, and nine months later, I gave birth to my son, Justin.

At 19 and with two babies and a barely there husband, I still didn't really know what I was doing. My marriage had gotten worse. I had no help with anything. Not the house, not the kids. It was all up to me to make sure everything was taken care of. Cooking, cleaning, bills — everything. Even though there were two small children devouring my attention every minute while they were awake, I felt alone. And sad. Every waking minute, I wondered what I could do better so that Mark would come home from work on time and talk to me. I just wanted him to help with dinner or interact with me and the kids. I spent most nights in bed alone because he would pass out on the sofa with no conversation prior. He didn't care how my day went, and there were maybe three sentences exchanged between us all night.

After I bathed both kids and got them into bed, I lay in the dark with silent tears of inadequacy and loneliness rolling down my face. I would say the prayer Gram taught me, so I wouldn't feel so abandoned. Sometimes it consoled me enough so I could fall asleep, but I would have horrible dreams that woke me in the middle of the night. Terrors of what I had escaped, waking myself up with my screams. Sleeping through them was impossible, and I was falling deeper and deeper into a dark depression.

I hadn't lost any of the baby weight. In fact, it was just the opposite. I had gained more weight after Justin was born. Eating was the only thing that made me feel good. It was the only thing I did just for me. But it was a love-hate relationship. I was up to 250 pounds. I wouldn't look in the mirror, but I always had a soda and candy bar close by. I felt like a disgustingly fat cow, and I was so lonely.

Chapter 26

Mom was on her way over for dinner, uninvited. She called one afternoon and told me to make fresh coffee because she would be over to see the kids. I hung up the phone, wishing I had the courage to tell her not to come, but I didn't. She would invite herself over at least once a week, and I would serve her coffee and a meal. She spent the time at my house criticizing my parenting, home, and how I looked and all the while smoked at the kitchen table even though I had asked her not to. She never played with the kids or helped with a meal. She was just another mouth that I was expected to feed.

"Don't you have any fresh coffee?" she asked, as she barged in.

I knew I should stand up for myself, but instead, I just went to the counter and started a fresh pot. I buried my self-loathing with a grocery store cookie I had failed to resist buying that morning. The box was already half empty.

As with most nights, Mark was still at work, Justin was happily waving a rattle on his blanket in the living room, and Jessica was just underfoot, as one-year-olds usually are. Jessica yanked Justin's pacifier out of his mouth and inserted it into her own. He let out a wail of discontent.

Mom, oblivious to the kids, announced, "You're getting fat."

I walked across the living room to pick up Justin and balance him on my hip, while handing Jessica a board book. I could feel her watching me as I walked past her, feeling very self-conscious of my body and wishing I were invisible.

"I'm starting a new diet," I lied.

I plucked the pacifier out of Jessica's mouth and put it back into Justin's. Mom laughed at me and said, "Well, your ass is as wide as this house. It better be one hell of a diet."

Mark didn't come home that night, which had become the norm. After Mom left, I sat watching TV and finished off the box of cookies plus a two-liter bottle of Pepsi, the leftovers, and a peanut butter and jelly sandwich before going to bed. *She's right*, I thought. *I'm a fat cow.*

By the time Justin was a year and a half, I was completely miserable. One night, I was lying in bed, almost asleep, when Mark opened the door and lay down on his side of the bed. I took him coming to our bed that night as a sign that he missed what our life was like in the beginning. *Maybe he does still love me*, I prayed as he lay on the bed. But it was the opposite. When I tried to touch him, he rolled all the way to the edge of his side, almost falling out of bed.

"I deserve better than this," I sobbed. "Do you want me to leave? Because I'll leave," I threatened.

"Who will want you? You're a cow," he said and passed out.

By then, I was 300 pounds and failing at my diet (just like my mother said I would). It's not like Mark was in shape — or even attractive. Nonetheless, I believed every horrible word he said to me. On another night, he came into our room where I was lying in bed. Apparently, he was drunk, which allowed him to touch me, and I felt so lonely and inadequate that I let him.

Chapter 27

A few weeks later, I found out I was pregnant. What would have been the point of birth control with a husband who wouldn't touch me? I wanted the marriage to be like it was at the beginning and was sure this baby was going to make Mark love me and want me again. Never did I think that it would make things worse.

I made a doctor's appointment without telling him, and when the doctor confirmed the pregnancy, the despair and loneliness I had felt for the past two years was replaced with joy and hope. *He will love me now*, I thought to myself as I drove home. I tried to think of ways I was going to tell him the great news. I'd make a special dinner. I wondered if this tiny baby was a boy or a girl. I was preoccupied just enough not to see a car that ran a red light. By the time I saw it, it was coming straight at me, and I had only a millisecond to decide whether I let it hit me or I run my car into a cement barrier and go over a bridge, so I let her hit me. When I came to, two EMTs were hovering inside my car.

Even though I was terrified that my baby may be hurt, I couldn't help feeling embarrassed when the EMTs opened the door of my car and saw me lying sideways in the front seat. When the first responder saw how fat I was, he looked surprised, annoyed, and disgusted.

"We need all hands on deck!" he called.

I felt like an injured whale hoping there were enough strong men to lift me onto the stretcher. Their attitude seemed more of disgust than helpfulness. They were trying to get me out of the car, and I was so scared because I knew that I had this tiny child in my body that I was trying to protect and was very aware that at any time, they could drop me and make my and my baby's injuries worse.

It took three people to get me out of the car. My face had hit the windshield, my knee had gone through the dash, my other knee had broken the stick shift, and my back was killing me. I kept telling them that I was pregnant and that I needed to save my baby, but they seemed more preoccupied by my size. They had the same look on their faces that I would get from a waitress when I would ask for a table instead of a booth, so I would fit. I kept saying, "Please help me, someone, please help me."

But there was no urgency to get me out of the car and to the hospital. When I was finally taken out of the car and brought to the hospital, I was left in the hall of the emergency room, lying on a hospital gurney in the ER waiting to have a test run with a C-collar on my neck. My head burned because it was in full contact with the metal gurney. I lay like that for hours.

Mark never showed up during this time. I had given the EMT drivers his number and asked them to call him. I was hoping he would come, but he didn't. Tears rolled down my face, stinging as they crossed over the cuts on my face. I was scared for my baby and felt like a fat slug that no one really cared about. Finally, the nurse came to collect me for X-rays and a CT scan.

"I'm pregnant," I told her, thankful someone was finally tending to me. I was so scared because I knew the radiation wasn't good for my baby.

"I know," she said. "But we have to see if you broke anything. It won't be good for your baby if you can't walk."

I knew she was right. The scans showed that I broke my nose, and my spine had hairline fractures. They said it was a compound fracture, which can be very painful and cause nerve damage. My whole face throbbed and felt three times larger than normal. I couldn't breathe through my nose at all. "But what about my baby?" I asked, not caring about my injuries. Technology in 1988 was not like it is now. Since I was only a few weeks pregnant, they really couldn't tell if the baby was all right or not.

"It's too soon to see a heartbeat," the doctor replied. I was crushed. All I wanted to know was if my baby was okay. I just wanted an answer, but the answer I got was one I didn't want to hear.

"You are probably going to miscarry," he continued. "The force of the steering wheel to your lower abdomen and pelvis was extreme." He reached down, lifted my hospital gown, and looked at the pad under my bottom. "I don't see any spotting yet," he said. "But nature will take her course soon. Even so, you'll need to stay on bed rest because of your back."

After the doctor walked away, I closed my eyes and prayed — hard. "Please, God. Don't take my baby," I chanted over and over. I was still in the emergency room with just curtains for walls, but I didn't care if anyone could hear me except for God.

I spent the next several hours in the ER. I could hear other patients moaning and coughing on either side of my curtain, and twice a nurse came in to check my vitals and lift my gown like the doctor had. "No spotting yet," the nurse said.

"That's a good sign, right?" I said. "Maybe my baby is okay." She put my gown back in place and squeezed my arm. The look on her face spoke volumes. "Your husband is on his way," she said, avoiding my question. She walked away and closed the curtain behind her.

After what seemed to be an eternity, Mark arrived. "Kim, there you are!" He said as he opened the curtain. I had dozed off, and his entrance startled me. Seeing a familiar face finally made my eyes swell with tears again. "I've been looking all over for you," he said. He sounded frustrated with the effort. "How bad is the car? What are we going to do?" he asked.

I didn't know how to respond to him. In that moment, I felt more alone than I ever had in my entire life. Even in the darkest moments with my mother, I understood that I didn't get to choose her. But I chose this man, and somehow, he cared more about our car than my life.

"They said I'll probably lose the baby," I finally mustered. This was not how I had planned on telling him. I was going to light some candles and set a relaxing mood before I announced the big news. Instead, my proclamation was given in a hospital, with dread and fear. His reply was incredulous.

"Wait, what? A baby? We don't need another mouth to feed. I told you this, Kim, when you brought up having another kid last year. It's probably best for everyone if you lose it. Who knows what will be wrong with it because of the accident anyways."

I tried to pretend that I didn't hear what he said. I hoped his reaction was because of the situation and not because he really meant it. I was sure that a baby would make him love us and want to be around us. After he left that day, he didn't come back to visit me while I was in the hospital, and each time we spoke during our few phone calls, he asked if I had lost it yet.

I was discharged a few days later. Mark and the kids showed up to take me home, only we didn't go home. On the way told me that he couldn't take care of me and the kids and work and that I would have to stay at my mother's.

"Like hell, I will!" I responded. That was not happening. But he insisted, and I was powerless to stop it. He was also right. My back was broken. I needed to stay in bed for both my back and the baby. How was I supposed to take care of two little kids while he was at work? And it's not like he was any help when he was home, either. It was a hot spring morning, and I stared out the window feeling the warm air from the open window whip the hair out of my face. *Look what you got yourself into, Kim,* I said to myself. *He doesn't want you anymore, and he is bringing you back to the place you hate the most.* I just stared out the open window until Jessica, who was sitting quietly in the backseat with Justin, said very quietly, "I missed you, Mama. Are you okay?"

I couldn't hold in the tears anymore. They came flooding down my cheeks, and I turned to see my beautiful reasons for life sitting in the back seat. "I missed you, too," I said and reached to grab her little hand. "Of course I'm okay! Mamas are always okay!"

I realized then that my kids were my everything, and if I had to go back to the hell I escaped so that I could lie in bed to try to keep this baby inside me safe, I was going to do it, God willing. When we pulled up in front of the house, Mark left the truck running and grabbed our son out of the back. I slowly opened the heavy truck door and got myself out. My body hurt so much. My back especially. If I moved too quickly or turned the wrong way even a little, I had a shocking, sharp, debilitating pain that took my breath away. By the time I got through the front door, with Jessica following in my footsteps, Mark was exiting the house. No hug goodbye. He just shut the door and was gone.

Just like that, I was right back to my nightmare. The house was the same, stinking of cigarettes and filth. Mom had set up her bedroom in the living room and was sitting in a filthy recliner when we arrived. Jessica clung to me as we stood there, Justin sat in his car seat that Mark had plopped on the living room sofa. Mark was gone, and I didn't know what I was supposed to do. The house was no place for small kids, but I hurt so bad I couldn't bend over to clear an area for them to play. There were piles of newspapers, dirty dishes, and trash covering pretty much every inch of the house, with only a path to the kitchen and another to the hall that led to my old bedroom and the only bathroom. She looked at us standing there and said, "Keep the kids out of trouble, and don't let them get into any of my stuff."

Jessica and I walked to my old room and opened the door. It was full of shit, just like the rest of the house. By now, my body was screaming in pain, and I had to lie down.

"Jessica, do you want to play a game?" I asked.

"Yes!" she said.

"Okay, let's see who can push more stuff off the bed first."

She loved the idea of making a mess, and this one was Mom-approved, so she dug right in.

"Can I stand on the bed, Mommy? Some of this stuff is heavy."

"Absolutely," I said. "Just make sure you push all the stuff off the bottom of the bed and not the side." I needed to make sure I could get up and out of the room without falling.

"Okay!" she giggled, and the crap went flying. Justin, thank goodness, was happy sitting in his car seat with his toy truck, nibbling on Cheerios. He was known to be like Houdini and get out of his car seat in a split second, but not today. It didn't take long for Jessica to win the game. All of the newspapers, bags of old magazines, clothing, and all the trash that had been on my old bed now was heaped at the foot of the bed on the floor.

"Great Job, Jess, you win!" I told her.

"What's my prize, Mama? She asked, smiling big from her win.

"Well, when we go to Walmart, you can pick any baby doll you want. How about that?" I said.

Her smile turned into a pensive frown. She wanted her prize now. I really just needed to lie down, though. "Hmm... how about a piece of bubble gum and a dollar instead?" She jumped off the bed and asked if the gum was in my purse. "Yup!" I replied. "You can get it and the dollar, too."

I found an old blanket that was still in my closet and laid it on top of the old mattress. I finally spoke to my mother and asked if she could keep an eye on Justin, who had fallen asleep in his car seat while Jess and I took a nap. She looked past me and asked Jess if she wanted to take a nap or watch the *Lady and the Tramp* with her. Jess went for the movie invitation. Mom was kinder to Jessica and didn't hit or demean her like she had me. However, she was very strict with and mean to Justin. Whenever she visited, she would always threaten to "beat his ass" if he didn't behave. Of course, I would never let that happen, though.

I went to lie down. When I woke up from my nap, I could hear him crying from the front room. He was crying so hard in his car seat that he could almost not catch his breath between sobs. I got up and went to him. "What's wrong?" I said and sat beside him on the sofa, trying to console him without picking him up. Mom proudly chimed in, "I beat his ass," she said. "Next time, he will think twice about climbing out of his car seat."

I had no words. I was still afraid of her. She walked past me and went to the front porch for a cigarette. Jess was still busy with her movie. I couldn't pick Justin up, but I stroked the top of his head and sang "You Are My Sunshine" quietly to him until he calmed down. That night when Mom went out to buy cigarettes, I called Mark and told him what happened. I begged him to come home. "You have to stay, Kim. I can't take care of you," he said.

The next few weeks were much of the same. My mother picked on Justin whenever he wasn't perfect. I ran interception as much as I could and kept him with me most of the time in my room. I was slowly healing, and the pain was now a dull ache — and I was still pregnant. Ten weeks to be exact. On the third week of my stay, I woke up to Justin crying in the front room again. He must have gotten out of the Pack 'N Play. I hurriedly went to see what was wrong. He was sitting on the floor crying, and Jess was trying to give him his toy truck to make him stop. "What's wrong?" I asked, gingerly picking him up off the floor.

"Grandma spanked him, Mama, so he would be a good boy today. She spanks him every morning to remind him to be a good boy. I'm always a good girl, so Grandma doesn't have to spank me to make me

156

remember like she does with Justin." Just then, my mother walked in, and I found my words. I was so pissed that she had been treating my son like this — like she had treated me.

"Why do you spank him every day?" I asked, not in a rage because I was still afraid of her, but confronting her at all was huge for me to do. Her response was matter-of-fact.

"He needs to learn not to be a little fucker," she said.

I immediately called Mark's work and told them there was an emergency, and he had to come *now*. No other explanation. I didn't quite hang up the phone because I knew he was going to call and try to tell me he couldn't come again, and I wasn't going to hear it again.

I told Jessica to help me get our stuff together because Daddy was coming to take us home. My mother's response: "Good, I'm tired of taking care of your fat ass."

Mark showed up about an hour later, asking where the fire was.

"I'm coming home now!" I said. "I can take care of myself and the kids. You don't have to worry about anything."

The ride home was silent. The days and nights that followed were pretty much the same as they had been. But I was still pregnant and determined to see this pregnancy through.

I drove myself to my obstetrician appointments. I slowly healed and took care of the kids, the trailer, and Mark. I also self-medicated my loneliness with food. The "I'm pregnant, so I can eat anything I want because it's good for the baby" justification gave me permission, but the food didn't heal my desolation. Taking care of me was not on the agenda. Changing diapers, washing laundry, and cleaning the trailer were my priorities.

When I passed by the bathroom mirror and saw my fat face and undone hair, they made me sick to my stomach. So I stopped looking. Reading *The Velveteen Rabbit* for the hundredth time and snuggling with my kids kept me going. Slathering my lower back with BenGay and watching my swollen belly move while I lay in bed was my nighttime ritual. Mark had checked out. He was barely home. But I kept telling myself that once this baby comes, it's going to be better. That was my new nighttime mantra.

Jordan, my third child, was born four weeks early. The doctor said it was best to deliver early than to put undue stress on my injured back. He was delivered via C-section on December 30th — healthy and 7 pounds 15 ounces. Mark stayed for the birth but disappeared right after and didn't come back until we were discharged. The heaviness of my depression grew. Postpartum depression also set in, and I cried all the time.

I knew I didn't belong to Mark anymore. He didn't want me and said so regularly. Trying to raise three kids under four was so overwhelming, all I wanted was to sleep. My mother was now in a relationship with an ex-con son of her neighbor's, too busy to bully me, too busy to help me. Not that she ever would. I called Mark's mom after I got home from the hospital with Jordan. She didn't live far, and I hoped she would want to help with her grandkids, even though she clearly despised me. When I first became pregnant with Jessica, she sternly reminded me that she was not going to be a built-in babysitter.

"You spread your legs, you make your bed," she said. But I took a chance because I was so fucking overwhelmed. When I asked her, she said, "Sorry, I have things to do. I have my own life, you know!"

I was living in a shitty trailer with three kids and a husband who was never around. I felt like fat white trash. I got myself into this, and it was my fault I was fat, that my husband thought I was horrific. I never again asked her or anyone for help.

Chapter 28

The marriage continued on a downward spiral as my weight climbed up. I would stay awake after getting the kids to bed. Every night I consumed a full two-liter bottle of Pepsi and a bag of Lays potato chips. I did this every night as I waited for Mark to come home. The food somehow made me feel happy, at least for a little bit. But by the time I went to bed alone, I was right back in my black hole of depression. *I will do better tomorrow*, I told myself. *Tomorrow, salads and water are all I will eat.* I made this promise every night and broke it every morning. It was a vicious cycle.

When I wasn't busy taking care of three small kids, my mind wandered, thinking how it would be if I could disappear. I even dreamed about throwing myself out of a moving car or stepping into traffic and letting the oncoming cars run me over. *No one would care*, I thought. *Everyone would be happier if I was gone anyway.* But just when it was almost impossible to get out of bed, Jessica would bring me a picture she had colored just for me, or Justin would come over and give me the biggest hug ever just because I found his toy truck under the sofa. Or Jordan would look at me with his big brown eyes and smile like there was no one else he wanted to see. Just his Mama. These tiny, beautiful miracles gave me the strength I needed to keep going. I knew I was needed.

Being needed wasn't enough, though. I hated myself and my life. I had no friends, and my kids were my life. By the time Jordan turned two, I was 403 pounds. I was so fat I couldn't lie flat to sleep because the weight of my chest on my lungs was too great, and I couldn't breathe. My legs rubbed together and wore holes in the thighs of my pants and made my skin raw. I could hardly find clothes big enough to fit me. Even my shoe size went up from a women's 10 to a 12. My feet hurt from walking on the circles of rubber, which were all that was left inside the soles of my shoes. We were too poor for me to buy new shoes every time they wore out, so I would fold paper towels to line the inside, but that only worked for a little while.

One night, instead of Pepsi, I decided to drink some of the wine that we had in the back of the refrigerator. I never had drunk before, and the wine hit me pretty quick. I turned off the TV and turned on the radio instead. I was awake when Mark came home this time. He was shocked to see me awake and immediately dodged into the bathroom. I had a pretty good buzz going, and it gave me courage.

"I'm not happy," I said to him once he came out of the bathroom. "I want to have a family that you are a part of and to feel like I matter to you. I need you to love me... please," I said.

"You're repulsive," he said.

"How can you be so mean?" I cried. "You want me to leave you? Because I will. You can't just ignore your wife and expect her to stay."

"Where are you going to go?" he scoffed. "No one wants a fat pig for a wife." He walked out the front door, and I grabbed the wine bottle.

Chapter 29

The next day, I had the worst headache ever. I kept going over what he said in my head and remembering the look on his face. *Maybe he's right,* I thought. That night, I was listening to music, sitting on the floor, folding a basketful of toddlers' clothes, when a familiar song came on that made me stop thinking about disappearing from the face of the earth. It was Gloria Gaynor's "I Will Survive."

There's a reason clichés become clichés. Even though I knew this as an adult, this was the song I played over and over in my head as a girl — before I even knew what a cliché was. This anthem for the marginalized and downtrodden quieted the fantasies about killing myself and stirred up questions about what I needed to do to not just survive but live.

I got up off the floor, grabbed a notepad and a pen, and made a to-do list. It turned out to be a pretty short, albeit difficult, list:

1. Lose weight.
2. Get a divorce.
3. Go back to school and get a college degree.

Mom had always told me I wasn't smart enough to go to college. I pushed her ever-present criticism aside because I realized I had nothing to lose. I had already experienced failure. I experienced it every time I looked in the mirror. Failing again wouldn't hurt me, but not trying to succeed would.

After I wrote these three life-changing action items, I no longer wanted to jump out of a moving car or eat a bag of chips and drink a two-liter bottle of Pepsi. I actually felt excited. I felt like my life was going to turn around, and I wouldn't end up like most people in my life thought I would — fat, poor, and just like my mother. I finished the laundry and went to bed, hatching my plan. I didn't think of new ways to take my life, and I didn't cry myself to sleep. I threw Mark's pillows on the sofa, locked the door, and slept like a baby.

The next day, unlike all the mornings after promising myself that I was going to change things and then just repeating my bad habits all over again, I scrambled two egg whites, drank some coffee, took a shower, and got the kids ready for school. Usually, I would start my day with a quart of chocolate milk and get the kids ready for school while still in my pajamas.

Then Jordan, who was four years old, and I would come home. He would play, and I would sit around with the Soaps on and snack on crap all day until the bus returned Jessica and Justin home. Instead, I put Jordan in his stroller, and we walked the circle road we lived on. Although my feet hurt, I felt exhilarated. I put him down for a nap, took a shower, blow-dried my hair, and attempted to put on some makeup.

On this day, my mother decided to come over, which she did about once a week. She could sense I was happy and wanted to squash it. As usual, she demanded her coffee and sat at my kitchen table while she told me that I was a bad mother and that my children were spoiled as I picked up their garage sale toys. Today was no different.

"You need to beat his ass, Kim. Show him who's boss," she said when Jordan dropped his toy from the high chair for the third time, and I picked it up for the third time. "Use the belt on his little ass, and the little son of a bitch will know who is in charge."

The idea of taking the belt to my beautiful son made my blood boil, but I kept my calm. I knew I had to.

"It's just a little game we play," I replied as I scooped him out of the highchair and took him to the other room. I lowered him into his playpen to keep him out of her view. Having her over was a very carefully choreographed dance with the devil. For some sick reason, I had this need to show her I was a great mom and loved my kids, but also the necessity to protect them from her venomous strike.

Walking back into the kitchen, I changed the subject and made the mistake of telling her that I was on a diet. "I've started a diet, and I'm doing really well. I even think my pants feel a little looser today, I added. She hadn't noticed that I was dressed in more than pajamas, and my hair was clean and styled. Instead of waiting for her response, I nervously went on. "It's a 1,200-calorie-a-day diet, and I think it's really starting to work."

"Where the fuck did you come up with this so-called diet?" she asked. I didn't tell her that I thought of it myself. Instead, I lied and said it was a diet my friend swore by. It was obviously a lie since I had no friends.

"It won't last," she said. "You're too weak and have never stuck to anything in your life."

I went to the back of the trailer to get more laundry. Her words stung and made me second-guess if I could actually do it. Maybe she was right. When I came back to the kitchen, she was gone. I suddenly felt less confident about my weight loss plan, and my courage started to turn into doubt.

Later that evening, after we had finished dinner, I saw her dented, gold 1975 Maverick pull into the drive from the kitchen window. The car had no muffler, and I could smell the emission smoke 20 feet away. Great, just when I thought she had left for the day, here she was on the front porch again. I had locked the door after the kids came in from the bus, and after trying the doorknob and realizing it was locked, she started to pound on it loudly. When I opened the front door, she had a McDonald's bag in her hand. She pushed it at me and said, "Here. There is a Big Mac and large fries in here for your dinner."

I stood there speechless. What the hell did this mean? For my dinner? She knew I had just started a diet. She turned around, got back in her car, and drove off without saying another word. After closing and locking the door, I held the paper bag in my hand, and a power came over me so strong that it was almost like what I did next was not really me doing it but a force stronger and more confident than I could be.

I walked over to the trash can, stepped on the black lever, and threw the bag of hate-filled sabotage away. That evening was the last time I second-guessed my ability to achieve my weight loss goal. All of my doubt was now replaced with a hunger, not to eat, but to be healthy and not obese anymore.

I was eating healthfully and knew I needed exercise, but my time to do so was very limited. I was also very self-conscious and knew if I could find time to go to a gym, I would be stared at and made fun of. It was bad enough being gawked at in the grocery store, so going to a gym was out of the question.

So I decided that when Mark did come home, which was always way after the kids were asleep, I would go for a walk. It may not sound like a big deal for most, but when you weigh just under 400 pounds and your thighs rub together all day long from tending to the kids and the trailer, by the end of the night, they were red and raw, so taking a walk was a painful ordeal, and I had to push myself to do it.

The first time I went out, I set a goal for myself. "Okay, Kim," I said to myself. "You need to walk to the street light without stopping."

It was hard, and more than once, my mind filled with doubt. By the time I was about 500 feet from my trailer, I wanted to turn back. But then I saw that damn McDonald's bag dangling from my mother's hand like Satan himself trying to tempt me. I saw her looking at me with the surety that I would fail, that I was a loser who never finished anything. So I turned up the volume on my Walkman, and I kept going.

"Three more driveways," I said to myself.

Once I got to the light, I made another deal with myself to increase the distance the next time and every time after.

The second time, I walked by six more driveways, and within a month, I could walk the entire circle of the trailer park. This was probably a quarter of a mile, but boy, did I feel like a champion athlete when I did it for the first time. My walking became a ritual that I looked forward to. Although I was restricted on the nights I could go based on when Mark came home, I made sure to be ready every night just in case he did.

Because my home scale only measured up to 300 pounds, I would use the scale that was at the Walmart pharmacy, next to where you could self-check your blood pressure. I would go every Wednesday to check my progress. The first week I was down eight pounds! I made sure that when I did check my weight, no one was around to see. Sometimes I had to circle back a couple times to make sure the coast was clear. By Week 3, I was down 23.5 pounds! The pharmacist behind the counter must have heard my "Yay!" when the red needle finally stopped at 376.5.

"Great job, and keep up the good work!" she said.

I guess the coast hadn't been clear after all. Her words caught me by surprise and filled me with joy.

After one month, I was down almost 30 pounds. My pants were baggy! I couldn't believe that I didn't have to lie on the bed trying to zip the largest pair of pants K-Mart sold, size 28. My legs rubbed together still, and the soles of my shoes still wore out, but not as quickly. I learned to sew patches over the holes in my pants where my thighs rubbed and bought insole liners and doubled them up to keep my feet from hitting the bare soles. Those tricks worked and made it easier to reach my next goal of walking around the park twice in one night. I was elated.

Eating more healthfully wasn't nearly as hard, I think, because Gram had never bought junk foods (except for the Reese's she hid in her crochet table and shared while we sat in front of the television as she crocheted her latest blanket). I grew up eating what the garden provided with a little meat and always homemade jams, breads, and juices. It wasn't until I moved in with my mother that I ate primarily processed and fried foods.

Mom had always claimed to be a great cook, but most of the time, we ate fried takeout when her Social Security checks came at the beginning of the month, and the rest of the month, we ate whatever came in a box and was four for a dollar. We stood in line every month for the government subsidies, which included cheese, canned meat, powdered milk, and peanut butter. But then she would sell it to the neighbor, along with her food stamps, for money to buy cigarettes and pills. She knew how to work the system, but I knew how to work. And I knew I could work hard enough to lose this weight.

Chapter 30

One day, Mark and his brother, David, were hanging out at a friend's house. The friend, Jeff, lived in the trailer across the street from us. He had just moved there a few weeks prior, and the three of them liked to stand around in Jeff's driveway, talking about trucks. Such was the case this afternoon as I walked out to get the mail.

"Hey, Kim," Jeff called out as I shut the mailbox. "Are you losing weight?"

This surprised me. Other than the cashier at the grocery store and the pharmacist, he was the only one who noticed. I nodded, beaming at the recognition.

"Looking good! Keep up the good work!" he called.

I was flattered. Words like this were never said to me. Not by Mark. Not by my mother. Not by anyone. Not ever.

Jeff started to come over more and more to hang out with Mark but chatting with me when he did. Every time he came by, he noticed my progress and told me how great I looked. I loved the attention and looked forward to his visits. They were innocent, but the attention was something I had yearned for, and it motivated me to keep going.

Mark had pretty much checked out, often not coming home at all, and when he did, he slept in the tiny piece-of-crap camper in the backyard. We fought when he was home — about money, the kids, and him never being around. Most of the time, all three topics were the meat and potatoes of these fights. He neglected the kids, and when they got in his hair, he would spank them. I was becoming stronger and more self-confident. Time to start Number 2 on my list.

I was providing daycare in our home and would stash what I could. One night, he came home late and was angrier than usual. The kids were tucked in bed, and I was on the sofa, dressed for my walk, waiting patiently for him to get home. As he walked in, I walked past him to go out the door.

"Where the fuck do you think you're going?" he asked.

I knew he was expecting to find his dinner in the microwave waiting for him like every other night.

"Make your own dinner," I told him. "I'm going out." I'd had enough of his sour mood.

He pushed me into the wall as I tried to get past him, grabbing my arm and pinning me to the wall. I was able to wiggle free, and although I wasn't hurt, I was scared and pissed at the same time. I knew I was done with this marriage.

"I want a divorce," I growled at him.

"Ha!" He laughed and pushed past me out the front door. I followed him, screaming over and over that I was leaving him. He ignored me and took off in his truck. I went back in the house, fuming. I opened the drawer for a notepad and paper and ferociously wrote him a letter, telling him I was done. We were getting divorced, and I would move out as soon as I could. I marched outside and taped it to the camper door. He didn't come home that night, but when I looked the next evening, it was gone, so I knew he'd read it.

I kept the money I had been stashing in the toe of a tube sock in my underwear drawer. By now, I had saved $400. This wasn't enough for a deposit and the first month's rent, but I was getting there and should have enough in a couple of months. My sock money kept my hopes up and me sane as I continued to deal with his shit.

Jeff came over a couple days later. Mark was gone, and I was home alone with the kids. We started to talk, and I broke down and told him everything that was going on, the abuse, the name calling, all of it. It was like a dam broke, and I couldn't stop. I felt so raw and naked after I told him everything, and he was so kind and caring.

"Kim, you deserve better than this," he said. "You are a great mom and a beautiful person." His words pulled me in, and I was hooked. "If I was lucky enough to have someone as beautiful as you, I would treat her like a princess and protect her from the world."

Suddenly, I saw him differently than I had in the past. As weeks went by, we talked on the phone almost every day. He stopped by a lot to play with the kids and give me a break. He gave me compliments all the time. "Wow, Kim, you look more beautiful than ever," he would say every time I saw him. He was so encouraging as I lost more weight. We didn't really date, but I would spend time with him after the kids went to sleep. We got very close very quickly, and he knew I planned on moving out as soon as I saved up enough money.

We became so close he asked me to move in with him. I didn't want to live down the street from Mark, so we searched and found a twin home not too far away, and he sold his trailer. I dreaded telling Mark that I was leaving, but I also couldn't wait to do it.

Finally, the day arrived. I sat in our living room, waiting for Mark to come home. Jeff was waiting for me in his car down the block. He even offered to come over, so we could do it together. But I was afraid of what could happen, so I said I would do it alone and come right over after.

As soon as Mark walked into the house, I stood up and said, "I am moving out with the kids. I'm divorcing you." I told him my plans and that I had been seeing Jeff. He came unglued. He swore at me and called me a cheater even after I reminded him that I had asked for the divorce months earlier. This didn't help. In fact, he became super jealous, begging me not to leave.

"You are my family, not Jeff's," he kept saying. "Please don't go. I can change." He put his head in his hands and just kept saying these two sentences over and over. I don't think he even noticed that I had gathered the kids from their room until I opened the front door.

"Why is daddy crying?" Jess asked as we walked outside. I didn't answer. At this point, I wanted him to feel the hurt and pain I had felt over the last four years of our marriage.

Instead, I said to her, "Come on, let's go get some ice cream."

Jeff pulled up as he saw us walking to the driveway, and off we went for a frozen treat.

Mark's pleas had no bearing on me. I had finally felt real love and was being treated well. And with my weight still dropping, I was down to 320 pounds, and I felt better about myself than I ever had. Just like that, I had jumped to the second item on my list, and once I ripped that Band-Aid off, I felt free.

I couldn't move all our things out that day because the townhouse wasn't available for another week. This made things in the trailer with Mark super uncomfortable and awkward. I spent the week focused on packing. Mark thought this was his shot to try to win me back. He came home right after work, bringing flowers and playing with the kids as soon as he walked through the door.

Little Jordan clung to me when his dad tried to get him to play because it was so foreign and fake. Even a three-year-old was smart enough to not trust him. Jessica and Justin were uncomfortable as well. I could tell by their reactions to his forced jovial mood, but they joined in halfheartedly for a little while. Then they went to their rooms after a few minutes of him joking around and playing.

I started hauling boxes to the twin home that Friday. Since we were not taking much, everything was moved in by Sunday. When I went to get the last load, I opened the front door of the trailer to find Mark sitting in the chair with a shotgun in his lap. I stopped dead in my tracks.

"What the hell are you doing?" I screamed. Jessica and Justin were standing behind me, still on the front porch, and Jordan was in my arms.

"If I can't have you, no one else will," He said very calmly. He was staring off into space. He didn't even look at me. And that scared me even more than if he had looked me in the eye. He seemed out of it, dazed and in a weird trance, which meant he could do anything. I turned and slammed the door behind me. I shoved the kids into the backseat of the car and peeled out as fast as I could.

Chapter 31

When they say history repeats itself, they are spot on. We repeat behaviors, both bad and good, and make the same mistakes over and over again, like a wind-up toy that keeps running into a wall.

Moving in with Jeff was pretty uneventful. We were busy adjusting to school and work schedules, and the kids were getting into their new routines. I was still losing weight, and I felt better about myself with every pound I shed. I had lost 200 pounds by the time we married the following year and was down to a size 18.

My mother was still in the picture. Despite everything, I was still hoping one day she would tell me who my biological father was, so I could find him. Ever since our conversation in the car on our trip to Kansas from Connecticut, I'd wondered about him and hoped I could find a way to contact him. She used the identity of who my father was as a carrot to keep me from completely walking out of her life.

She would say things like, "Your father came to town to see you, but I wouldn't let him in on more than one occasion." At first, I thought she was lying just to get my goat, but as I got older, I began to wonder more and more. What if he had come to find me, and she sent him away? What if she told him lies about me and he never wanted to meet me because of them? The one thought that never left my heart was, What if he wants to find me, get to know me, and be my dad but doesn't know where to find me? These what-ifs ran through my mind — all the time.

My mother ended up marrying the neighbor's ex-convict son, Don. She was nice to me after she was married, and I tried to build a relationship with her. Jessica was eight, Justin was seven, and Jordan was five when they were married.

This quasi-normal relationship she tried to build featured a weekly meal she would make for us to come and eat. I was hesitant to let my kids be around Don because he had been in jail. I asked why he had gone to jail, and her response was that he had been arrested at 19 for marijuana possession. According to her, he was hanging out with the wrong crowd. I was still leery and had a bad gut feeling, but Jeff said that everyone makes mistakes, and Don had paid for his. When we visited, Don always had gifts for the kids, and Mom had stopped calling me names and was civil. It was the nicest she ever was to me.

I was starting to believe that maybe we had a semi-normal relationship. Jeff, the kids, and I visited and had weekend dinners for roughly a year. And then, one day, I got a phone call from the police telling me that Don had been arrested on allegations of molesting the daughter of my mother's friend. They asked if I was aware that he was a known child molester. They asked about my children. When was the last time they were around Don? Have I noticed behaviors that were different from them when they were around Don? They felt they needed to warn me since my children had been around him. He was always so friendly around the kids when they would come by, and not once had I ever thought he was a predator. Worse (but not at all surprising), my mother had lied to me. She knew his history all along.

I immediately called my aunt Helen, freaking out, afraid that my children had been molested. I didn't have anyone else I could turn to. She still lived in Connecticut, and over the years, we had kept in distant contact. I didn't know what to do. I asked my three kids questions a parent shouldn't ever have to ask — if he had touched them inappropriately or made them do something that made them feel bad or uncomfortable. All three said no, but I was still worried that he had done something to my babies.

I blamed myself for not protecting them, for not knowing or seeing the signs that he was a child molester, and for thinking that my mother would ever be honest. I definitely should have known she wouldn't protect her grandchildren or any children she had in her home if it meant she could have the attention of a man, even the scum-of-the-earth kind of man.

My aunt flew out a couple of days after he was arrested and stayed with me. I met her at the airport and was greeted with a much-needed hug. She went to my mother's house a couple of times to do damage control. I didn't go with her, and she understood why. She tried to find out exactly what had happened and what was going to happen next with him. She wasn't really close to my mother, but whenever anything went wrong, she was always the one my mother reached out to. She stayed at my house, and that first night we stayed up talking. She asked me why I still had anything to do with my mother, asking me why I still let her treat me as badly as she did.

I really didn't know if Aunt Helen knew how she had treated me as a child, mainly because I had always made myself scarce or played with my cousin. But she could see it now.

I had been an emotional wreck since the police had taken him away. My hair was falling out, and I had a rash all over my body from the stress. I replied to her question honestly. "I'm afraid of her, but she is the only one who knows who my dad is. And I keep hoping that if I am nice enough, one day she will tell me."

This opened the conversation up, and I felt like I could trust her. I needed to tell someone what I had hidden for so many years. So, as warm tears flowed down my face, I told her the horrors of my childhood. And all throughout my story, I repeated, "I need to find my dad. Maybe he is different and will love me. Maybe he doesn't even know that I exist."

She reached over and gave me a soft hug after I was finished talking. But she looked at me, confused. "I thought your mother told you," She said. "She told us years ago when your stepdad was still alive, and I was there the night you were conceived."

I was dumbfounded. She knew who my father was? And she's known for all this time? And she never said anything to me. She must have never told him about me because I was sure that he would love me if he knew I existed.

She explained, "When your mom was 17, and I was 11, we went to babysit for our uncle one night. He had a two-year-old son and was going to the bars. He came home late, and your mother made me go to bed on the sofa before our uncle had returned. I woke up to the sounds of laughing and other sounds that I didn't know. I got off the sofa and saw your mom and our uncle making out in his room. I had startled your mom by saying something to them, and she told me to 'get my ass back on the sofa and don't get up again.' Then she shut the bedroom door. Years later, after your mom had married your stepfather, she told me that that was the night you were conceived. Our uncle is your father."

I sat there in disbelief, my mind spinning. I saw this uncle once. I sat outside his trailer for a whole day as my mother was inside talking to him. I kept trying to process what Aunt Helen had told me, and then the horrible truth sank in. My father was my mother's uncle, my grandmother's brother, and I was a product of incest. My dreams of finding my father were now shattered with the knowledge of who he was. I knew now that I was never going to put my arms around my daddy and hug him or tell him I loved him. The reality was that my mother got drunk and fooled around with her uncle willingly, and I was the mistake that came from it. I knew enough about the genetic issues that resulted from incest. I also knew that it was a shameful thing to be a product of, and I felt that shame as I looked at myself in the mirror the next morning.

This uncle, the one we had gone to visit, had died the year after. All of my hopes and dreams of ever meeting my father were now dead as well, and all I was left with was a mother who wished I had never been born, and now I knew why.

Aunt Helen visited with Mom the next day before she had to go home. She confronted her about me not knowing about my father and told her that she had told me everything. They argued, and Mom was pissed at her for telling me. That afternoon was the last time they saw each other. Years later, I asked Helen if she missed her, and she quickly responded, "Not at all... You weren't the only one she abused."

I called my mother a couple of days after Helen left and told her that I wanted to meet and talk. We agreed to meet at a local sandwich shop the following day, and Jeff took the day off, so he could sit a few tables away in case I needed him. I had filled him in on everything, and he wanted to make sure nothing happened to me. Jeff was very protective of me and always made sure he was the one to protect me from everything. Even though he was coming with me, I still very much felt like I was on my own. On the drive there, I prepared myself to face her, building my armor and my mind for when she would come at me. Because I knew she would.

I sat silently in the car as we drove to the diner, wondering what I was going to say to her. The fear I had felt as a child and adult had been replaced with anger and tenacity. I was no longer afraid to speak up to her, and my mind had a thousand red balls bouncing around in it with things I wanted to say to her, questions I deserved to have answered truthfully, and pain that I needed to end.

She was already at the diner when we arrived, sitting in a booth, smoking a cigarette with a cup of coffee in front of her. Her back was to me as I walked toward the booth, and she didn't turn to see me as I walked by and sat down. Her face was set in stone with no expression, and as I sat down, she looked at me with eyes full of anger and hatred.

176

All of the things I wanted to say were stuck inside my head, so I just sat there as she stared at me. She took a sip of her coffee and a drag of her cigarette. Finally, she broke the silence.

"My sister, the bitch, had no right telling you anything. It was none of your Goddamn business."

And like that, the dam broke, and all of the red balls of things I was going to say came rushing out fast and furious.

"None of my business!?" I said. I was loud enough that Jeff stood up from his table, ready to intervene. But he just stood there and watched as I continued on. "You knew how much I wanted to know who my father was. You knew how much I wanted to find him. You lied to me about all of it. You said a man got you pregnant and joined the marines because he didn't want me. You took me to my real father's house after Ritchie was murdered and made me sit outside, never even letting me meet him. Why did we even go there? What was the purpose of taking me there in the first place?" The words came out of my mouth freely and with ferocity. I demanded her to be accountable and finally tell me the truth. No more lies and bullshit.

She looked at me and said, "I went there because he owed me money. You were his, and he had a responsibility to give me money to feed you and buy you clothes. He was a bum, and he didn't have any money, so I told him to go to hell. I wasn't going to let him meet you unless he gave me money. You were better off not meeting him anyway. I did what I had to do, and one day you will understand."

"Understand?!" I was beside myself. "No, I won't understand how you slept with your uncle. No, I won't understand why you beat me! No, I won't understand why you lied to me about who my father was!" By this time, I was bawling uncontrollably. I could hardly look at her; I hated her so much. She just sat there and watched me fall apart. She said nothing, but she looked at me like I was weak. She despised me. I could see it in her eyes.

I calmed myself down and said quietly, "I can become ill with horrible diseases because of who he was, because of the genes being too close. Don't you understand that?"

I will never forget her reply or the crooked smile on her face when she delivered it.

"I always told you that you looked like my side of the family."

At this, I stood up to leave. The tears had stopped, and now my face was the one set in stone. I looked straight into her pathetic face. I was no longer intimidated by her.

"I never want to see you again," I said. "Don't ever call me or come to my house, or I will have you arrested."

These were the last words I said to my mother — and the last time I saw her alive.

Chapter 32

I never looked back after that day. I tucked all of the bad memories of my childhood in a closet, far back in my mind. The only thing I couldn't run away from was knowing that I was an embarrassment to the human race, something people joked about — the epitome of stupid. This stigma haunted me, and I always worried that I would get sick with an autoimmune disease or cancer.

No longer having my mother in my life was a good thing, though, and I was stronger for it. I was 28, newly married, 180 pounds and falling, and happy. I felt better than I ever had in my life. We lived in a house we bought in Wichita. Jeff's family accepted me, and I loved being part of his family. We attended church, my kids were adjusting to the new marriage, they were in scouts, and everyone seemed to be doing better than ever. For the first time since I was a small child with my grandfather, I felt like I was where I belonged.

My kids and I started to see what normal was like. I had taken the required courses and background checks with the state to run a preschool and daycare in our home, but I yearned to get my degree and become a nurse. I felt like I had so much to give and wanted to help people.

So, after speaking to Jeff, I enrolled myself at the community college in Wichita and started my college journey — Number 3 on my list. Of course, it was just the basic prerequisite classes, but I was on my way and loved every minute of it, especially my writing class.

Jeff had no children of his own, and since he seemed so good with my kids and I loved being a mom, we decided we wanted to try to have a child. But first, we met with a doctor that specializes in genetic disorders. I had to make sure that there would be no chance the baby

179

would have issues. Telling him about my bloodline was humiliating, but he was very assuring and kind when he explained that the chance of incest causing genetic issues was nonexistent. The chance of abnormalities had stopped with me.

It took more than a year to have a successful pregnancy. At age 30, after losing a pregnancy early on with twins, I gave birth to a perfect, beautiful ten-pound boy. We named him Jake, and our family felt complete.

About a year after Jake was born, Jeff was laid off from his job as a computer IT specialist. A few weeks later, he was offered a job in the small town of Abilene, Kansas. It was almost two hours away and much more rural than Wichita — if that's even possible. Since there were no other jobs around, we moved. I was still doing daycare and had no problem getting new clients.

We quickly found our place in the small, tight-knit community. Jessica, Justin, and Jordan were now 13, 12, and 10, and Jake was 1. I started to notice some teen angst with Jessica and Justin.

They had started arguing with Jeff, the cause of which I presumed was a mix of adolescence and a new environment. Overall, we had settled in nicely to our life in Abilene, and we were happy.

Chapter 33

Shortly after moving to Abilene, I found myself unexpectedly pregnant. I was surprised by this, given our difficulty conceiving Jake. I bought two tests, and both were positive, not just faint lines down the middle to make one question if it was really there, but dark pink lines that seemed to say, "Oh yeah, girl. You are definitely pregnant." First, I was shocked. Then, I was terrified. I sat in the bathroom staring at the tests for over an hour before Jeff came home.

The fighting had grown between him and my kids. In particular, he had started to pick on Justin and Jordan. He had a way of belittling them and always found something they had done wrong, no matter how hard they tried to do it right. Jordan kept out of the way, but Justin was more rebellious and knew how to push Jeff's buttons; because of this, he took the brunt of the abuse. Jeff treated Jessica differently, however. He always wanted to buy her gifts and things she liked. Although they argued, he vied for her approval and attention.

My boys were not perfect, but they were great kids doing normal things that boys do as they're growing up. One time, they needed batteries for their handheld video games and cassette players. They asked Jeff for some, but he gave them the third degree. "What happened to the batteries you had? How much are you using those things?"

To make matters worse, he was a control freak. A simple answer was never enough; he wanted every detail explained as to why anything happened, and he was the same with me. Ultimately, we just stopped saying what was going on because of all the questions: *Why? How come? Why didn't you?* It was too much. I didn't realize it then, but I was starting to lose who I had worked so hard to become. I was losing my identity and doing a disservice to my children for not stopping the insanity when it started.

And now I was sitting in the bathroom trying to figure out how this unplanned pregnancy happened. How was I going to explain it? That was the hardest part because the simple answer was *never* enough.

The proclamation of being pregnant again wasn't as bad as I had expected it to be. He asked only 20 questions, and then he was happy about having another mouth to feed. I just answered, "I have no idea," every time he asked me how this could have happened after everything we'd gone through to have Jake. He finally accepted the fact that there was a baby on the way, even though there was no scientific explanation as to why. And everything went back to normal, tumultuous as that was.

Nothing was normal about this pregnancy, though, and I knew it immediately. It was different than all of the others, and I was constantly worried something was wrong. I was right to worry. At 25 weeks, I had a brown discharge and was admitted to the hospital. The doctors managed to hold off the delivery until 26 weeks, at which point, things went south for me very quickly. I started losing an obscene amount of blood. My heart stopped twice. I was on a ventilator and went in and out of consciousness. At one point, I heard a voice tell me, "It's going to be okay."

There was no one around, and I knew it was God carrying me through this. In the brief moments I was awake, all I could think about was my baby, wondering if she was okay.

When I finally woke up for good, my head was clearer. They had put me on a ventilator and told me to cough as they pulled the tube out of my throat, through my mouth. It was painful and uncomfortable, and my throat felt really sore. The doctor came in during his rounds.

"You scared the shit out of me," the doctor said after they took me off the ventilator. "It's a miracle you're alive." I thought it was odd for a doctor to say that to a patient. He was in his mid-thirties with tons of dark brown hair. His eyes were a soft green, and he had a five o'clock shadow. "How's my baby?" I asked.

"You lost a lot of blood. You're very lucky to be alive," he repeated.

I wasn't quite grasping what had happened. He tried to explain. My placenta had grown scar tissue from my previous C-sections and attached itself to my bladder, where it grew until my bladder couldn't accommodate it anymore. My placenta started to detach from my bladder, filling my abdomen with blood that pooled and finally busted open with a vengeance.

Even though the doctor repeatedly tried to impress upon me the gravity of my situation, I just couldn't grasp it right then. All I could think of was my baby. We had chosen the name Julia Grace for her because I knew early on that if she survived, it would be by the grace of God. And now, that grace was evident.

"How's my baby?" I asked again. "And when can I see her?"

Chapter 34

When it was time to meet Julia Grace, it took everything I had to get out of my bed and into the wheelchair. I was so very weak, and any movement was a lot of effort. My daughter was almost five days old, but I had been awake for only a few hours. My nurse, a middle-aged woman who had a kind smile and smelled like Chanel, rubbed lotion on my feet after I settled into the wheelchair. She combed my hair and said, "You are going to meet your daughter for the first time. We need you looking your best."

As she pushed me through the dark NICU, all I could see were monitors with bright red and blue numbers. Alarms were going off, and babies were lined up in plastic cubes with IV lines and tubing coming from them. As I got close to Julia's incubator, I could feel the heat coming from it. I was not prepared for what I saw next, and the sight of her was so gut-wrenching I almost threw up. In front of me was this beautiful, yet scary, tiny creature.

She was smaller than any baby I had ever seen, her skin almost transparent. Her ears were so tiny they were practically nonexistent. She wasn't on the ventilator anymore, but she did have a tiny cannula running under her nose. The tears ran down my face as I looked at this beautiful little alien.

"I will take care of you. I promise," I said over and over. "Please don't die, Julia Grace. Mama's so sorry she couldn't keep you inside any longer."

Two days later, I was still so weak from the blood loss I could hardly walk. My doctor came in to check on me. "How are you feeling, Kim?" he asked as he pulled a chair up to my bed. I lied. "I feel good, a little tired. But almost as good as new. When can I be discharged?" Julia was still in the NICU, but I needed to be with her as much as I could.

"I need to be able to take care of my baby, to be there for her," I said. He sat there, and after a few moments, struck up a deal, thinking he would win and I would stay in the hospital a few more days.

"If you can get up and walk to the door and back by yourself, I will discharge you with the condition that you come to my office every day to have your blood levels checked."

I slowly got up from the bed. I stared at the door, memorizing how far away it was as I made my way toward it, sweat beading up on my forehead. Every step felt like my feet had cement shoes on. Just as I reached the door, the room started to dim, and I knew I didn't have much time before everything turned dark, so I turned around and walked back to my bed as quickly as I could. Thank God it was a straight shot. The room got darker with every step I took. By the time I walked the eight feet back to my bed, I couldn't see anything and hoped no one noticed my exhaustion and blindness. I rolled onto the bed once I felt it on the front of my legs.

I was released just as he promised. I stayed at the Ronald McDonald House for nine and a half weeks. It was located in the same parking lot as Julia's hospital, and as Julia grew, I recovered too. I slept a lot and had to have a wheelchair to go more than a few feet. I experienced lots of sweating, nausea, and blurred vision, but I was able to see Julia and my family as much as my body would let me.

When I visited her, I would sit in front of her isolette for the first few weeks and sing to her. I cried through most of the songs because I felt so helpless, and I was scared she was going to die. She was too tiny to hold, but I was there for her every day. Jeff came in on the weekends, and we both went to visit and spent hours next to her.

Finally, I was able to hold her. They laid her on my chest, skin-to-skin. I felt her tiny breaths and tiny movements, and I thanked God for saving both of us. He had promised everything would be okay, and He had kept His promise.

Julia grew and got stronger every day. She was downgraded to a hospital only 35 miles from where we lived. She was able to come home a week later, weighing a whopping four pounds. She and Jessica shared a homecoming that day. Julia came home, and Jessica had her freshman homecoming dance in high school. It was such a good day.

Chapter 35

About a month after Julia turned two, 9/11 happened, which resulted in Jeff's company starting to struggle. It was a horrible time, with so much fear and sadness throughout the country and our community. Everyone was terrified of more terror attacks, and there were news reports about anthrax in the mail. We were all on edge, and the economy was struggling under the lack of stability. Jeff was able to find a new job, but it was in Phoenix. We decided a move might be best for all of us.

Moving from a small town in Kansas to a large city made Jeff increasingly insecure, and he took it out on me and my kids. I had started making friends and had lost what little baby weight I had gained. We were in a new place, and after surviving Julia's birth, I was more confident than I had been before. For one or both of these reasons, our marriage got worse. He wouldn't take me out to eat without the kids. We didn't do anything as a family. The more weight I lost, the more insecure he became.

He said, "I feel like I'm taking a lamb into a lion's den. Men watch you, and I know what they're thinking."

If I went to the store, he made me take the kids with me, and I would have to call him once I got there and when I left. His relationship with Justin got worse. Jeff would fight with him, call him horrible names and push him across the room. With Jessica, though, he was the polar opposite, still always wanting to buy her things and vying for her attention, but she never wanted to be around him.

One day, I went to wake her up for school. I tried to open her bedroom door, but she had pushed her dresser in front of it. I freaked out.

"What's going on?" I demanded.

"I just don't want anyone coming into my room," she said.

"Who are you afraid of coming into your room?" I asked.

She wouldn't elaborate, but of course, I knew. This was the moment I realized I'd failed my children. I didn't know the extent to which I had failed them — and I intended to find out — but I knew that I had failed at the one thing I had always promised to do. Asking Jeff about it was out of the question. His obsessive behavior was too much to handle. Justin had already asked to move in with Mark back in Kansas.

Out of desperation to protect him from Jeff and his abuse, I agreed. It wasn't perfect, but Justin was 15, and I felt he could handle Mark easier than Jeff.

I sank into a deep depression. Somehow, I was right back where I had been so many times before — broken, abused, and sleeping on the bathroom floor because it was the only room with a lock on the door. I stayed in this depressed state for about a year. I was haunted by my daughter's dresser in front of the door. I was horrified that I hadn't been strong enough to act on the signs of abuse toward the boys when they were right in front of me. Why didn't I question more? Why didn't I insist on getting to the bottom of it? Why didn't I listen to my own intuition? And most important, why didn't I leave?

My one job was to protect my kids. When my mother beat me, in addition to her hateful disdain for me, she would always add, "Someday, you will be the same as me. You think you are better than me, but you are a piece of shit, just like I am." When I failed my kids, I heard those words and saw her face. She was both right and wrong at the same time. She was a strong, mean piece of shit. I was a weak, naïve piece of shit. After all I had gone through, I still had no voice. I still thought the only person who did bad things was her. But strong or weak didn't matter. The result was the same for my kids.

Just as it was Jessica's cry for help that sent me to the bathroom floor, it was her next cry for help that pulled me up off of it. She came home one day, and her pain and her truth about what was happening to her just exploded. And it was at this moment that I found my voice. I found the strength I didn't know I had.

This strength helped me get through a long and messy divorce. This strength helped us survive when I became a single mom with five children (four at home) and three jobs, so I could put food on the table and pay bills. Justin still lived with his dad in Kansas I had hoped he would return, but he didn't.

Chapter 36

I am not going to say that I always made the right choices navigating my way through this period. I dated a few people, all of whom taught me what I did and didn't like in a relationship. I was experiencing things young people do as they "try people on," except I was a mother of five and came with baggage. I called it "Louis Vuitton baggage," but there was no disguising the fact that it was a lot for anyone to take on in a new relationship. I dated one man who wanted me but not the whole family thing. I dated one who had his own kids and baggage. That was just too much. We ended up arguing about whose kids were better and whose were worse.

Then one night, when I was working one of my three jobs as a cocktail waitress in a restaurant whose clientele was primarily older, more prominent people — doctors, lawyers, and businessmen — a very tall, handsome man walked into the bar area and sat down. I noticed him immediately and watched as he sat alone, ordering a beer. I expected someone to come join him, and when no one did, I walked up and stood a few feet from him to give the bartender an order. I turned to him.

"You must be lost or from out of town because you are way too young to be in a place like this," I said.

He laughed. "I'm neither," he explained. I live close by and met someone here a couple weeks ago. I was hoping to see her again."

I was going through one of my mistaken relationships (I believed a man who said he was going through a divorce, except his wife wasn't aware of it). So it didn't bother me that this gentleman was so candid about looking for someone he had met a few weeks prior. Every time I came back to the bar, we would talk. I found out he was divorced, had a 10-year-old son, and a son that had died when he was four years old because of a brain injury that occurred during birth. I told him about losing my twins and almost losing Julia. And then I did what I would do to see if he ran away or not. I told him that I had five kids and worked a lot to support them. He listened to me and said, "Well, they are lucky to have a hard-working mom. And wow! You look great. I would have never guessed you had five kids."

It was a typical response for me. I had gotten pretty wise about guys, but he seemed different somehow. When he left, he asked me for my number. I never gave my number to guys who came on to me when I was working, but that night I did.

His name was Tim. He called a few times, and I ignored his calls. I had had time to think about why I had shared my number and chalked it up to a moment of weakness, forgetting that guys try to pick up women who work at bars all the time. I ignored his voicemails, and two weeks later, he came back to the restaurant. He was very persistent. So I decided to take a chance on him, and we started to date. This was by choice, not because I was looking for someone to rescue me, but because I felt connected to him and, eventually, his son.

The first time he met Jake and Julia, I was very nervous. I had exposed them both to my failed relationships, and I was leery of exposing them to anyone who might hurt them. It is very hard to date as a single mom. You want to be happy, but your little ones are affected by the choices you make.

We decided to meet at a family-owned Italian restaurant. Jake, Julia, and I arrived first, so we found a corner booth and waited. As soon as Tim walked to our table, both kids scooched over, with me squeezed in the middle, so I had no room on either side of me. He took a seat, and I made introductions. Then Julia grabbed the parmesan cheese shaker and started to lick the top as we were talking. Jake, who was seven, sat still and silent, but all of our attention was drawn to five-year-old Julia, who was completely oblivious to us.

Apparently, she was hungry. I was so nervous that Tim would be grossed out by Julia and would think that I was a bad mom for my daughter to do such a thing in a public setting, but his response was laughter and amusement.

The scene was light, and we all laughed as I asked Julia to put the shaker down because the food was almost here. Tim could tell both Jake and Julia were nervous and decided to tell a joke to break the ice. "Ever hear about the one-armed fisherman?" he asked.

This question caught both their attention. Jake, who had been fishing before, replied, "No..."

Tim slowly smiled and held one hand to the left. "The one-arm fisherman caught a fish this big," he replied. Jake got the joke immediately and started to laugh. Julia had no clue what was funny but laughed because everyone else did. The pizza came right after, and we enjoyed the meal.

A week later, I met Tim's son. I arrived at a Mexican restaurant, got a booth, and waited, a little nervous as to how his son would react to me and my kids. It was just me, Jordan, Jake, and Julia. Tim and Colin were 15 minutes late. Colin greeted me with a solid handshake and slid in across from me. As he did, I noticed that Tim was wearing mismatched flip-flops. They were the same style, but one was brown and the other black. When I pointed this out, it broke the ice. We were all laughing, and any nervousness I felt melted away as I watched the kids giggle at his mismatched shoes.

Our relationship grew — not just between Tim and me, but among the kids, too. It was very nice to be in a place where I wanted to be instead of one I had to be. On one of our weekends alone, while the kids were at their other parents', we took a quick getaway to California to visit Disneyland. I was very excited to have some alone time with him.

As we walked into the park, everything looked so fresh and new. A lot had changed since the last time I visited. However, one thing hadn't changed: the Haunted Mansion. We got in line without a second thought. But as we approached the front of the line, my heart started to beat a little faster, and the memory of riding it years ago started to flash in my mind. Not just memories of the ride but of the entire visit. Being pulled through the park to get to this ride, my mother's hand clenching my arm so hard she left bruises. I could feel those bruises again as I started to remember, and by the time we were at the front of the line to enter the spooky white mansion, I was in full panic mode, now unable to stop the flood of memories.

"Kim, what's wrong?" Tim asked. He had his arm around me like he was unsure whether to usher me onto the ride or out of the line altogether.

"Nothing," I said. I was too embarrassed to say anything more. But clearly, something was wrong. My breathing became fast, and my heart raced as we walked toward the ride. As the voiceover in the room started and the lights went out, I kept seeing my mother's face and the ticket holder looking at me in the dark, barely lit room, where I sat and begged to get off the ride.

I kept telling myself, *It's okay, don't lose it; you're not a baby anymore; it's going to be okay.*

The doors opened, and before I knew it, we were at the front of the line as we got into our "Doom Buggy." I became a child of seven, not seeing Tim beside me but seeing my mom — even though I did everything not to — standing on the platform, threatening the attendant and me.

I lost it.

I started to shake, closing my eyes so hard, trying to block out not only what was happening as the buggy traveled through the mansion but all the horrible memories only I could see. The ones that came pouring out of the vault buried deep in my brain, as clearly as the day they happened. Poor Tim.

"Please make them stop the ride," I begged Tim. "I want off!"

He had no idea what was going on. I hadn't told him anything about my mother other than I'd had a rough childhood. I had tried to share with him my childhood and what I went through, but after about 20 minutes of conversation and tears, he became annoyed and asked if we could not talk about it. "The past is the past," he said. "You need to move on and enjoy the present."

After that, I was too afraid to share anything because I knew his reaction would make me feel like I was stupid for not getting over it, and I just wanted to feel like I was normal and in a normal relationship.

On the ride, he just held my hand and kept saying, "It's not real. It's all fake, Kim."

He didn't laugh at my breakdown or make me feel bad. When the ride ended, he said, "It's over. You can open your eyes."

When I opened them, I was overcome by embarrassment. Two small children were laughing and talking about which ghost they were with. Their parents were laughing with them. I explained to Tim why I reacted the way I did, opening up to him about my one and only other time riding the Haunted Mansion. And somehow, he understood. Or he loved me enough to try because he was empathetic and made me realize that what happened in the past was in the past. But for me, that day was just as it was when I was seven, and although he held my hand and comforted me, I wished I could share with him, talk to him, and have someone understand me.

This trip happened right before we were married in July 2006. The following March, we took the kids to Disneyland, where we rode the ride again, this time as a family: Colin was 11, Jake 9, and Julia 7 — the same age I was the first time I went. The boys feared nothing and rode everything. Julia was more timid and had been afraid to go on most of the rides. But she was much braver than I had been and enjoyed the Dumbo ride and the other kids' rides.

When we got in line for the Haunted Mansion, I could see her looking at the large white mansion, trying to figure out just what kind of ride it was. There were no horses going up and down like the carousel or flying elephants that held a magic feather in their trunk flying round and round, up and down in the same circle. I held her hand and explained everything about the ride.

When we got to the front of the line, I said, "This is your chance to be brave with me. It is only make-believe, and I will be right there beside you." I was partly trying to convince myself of the same things. And then I said something that made us both better understand the fun of the ride.

"It's only *Scooby Doo* scary." I really don't know how that expression came to me but seemed to fit so well.

She looked at me, puzzled.

I went on, "You know how on *Scooby-Doo*, there are no real monsters, just pretend ones people have made to scare you? This is the same thing." And after I explained it that way, she was ready to ride the ride — still a little scared, but brave enough, and she trusted me enough to do so.

This time, I kept my eyes open the entire ride, and anytime I got scared or the memories tried to come back, I would say out loud, "This isn't real," and after the third time saying it, my sweet daughter, who now had her eyes open and was smiling ear to ear replied back "Nope, it's only *Scooby Doo* scary, Mama." And just like that, those bad memories were gone, and wonderful new memories were made. The vault was now open, and no heavy door was needed. And instead of darkness, there was light. Fear and pain were now replaced with love and happy memories.

And to this day, it's one of our family's favorite rides.

Chapter 38

As the years passed, our family made lots of fun memories. We loved big family dinners and coming up with fun dinner themes. The holidays were the best, too. I dressed up every Halloween with the kids and went trick-or-treating. Christmas was our favorite family holiday. Each of us had a special ornament that we placed on the tree each year. There were always lots of hugs and "love you's," and these were shared honestly and freely, always.

We had rough times, but we got through them together. And these rough times made us stronger, often laughing about them months after they had passed during one of our many weekend family dinners. I had built a beautiful family with my new husband, but the void of not having a Dad still lay heavy in my heart. I still worried about becoming sick because of my genes, and although I tried to push it out of my mind, I could never seem to. I hadn't heard from my mother since that day we met, when I told her that I never wanted to see her again. She never tried to find me — at least not that I knew of — and for that, I was thankful.

I did, however, discover that she had my cell phone number in a way I never expected to. The Friday after Thanksgiving in 2008, I was shopping for Christmas decorations, and I got a phone call from a Kansas area code. My heart stopped when I saw the number on the screen. All of my contacts from Kansas were saved on my phone, and the odds of a random call from Kansas during a holiday weekend were way too slim. I let it go to voicemail. *Please don't leave a message.* I kept thinking after the ringing stopped. I stood there in the middle of the aisle, fake Christmas trees on one side of me and light-up reindeer on the other, waiting to see if I received a voicemail.

Minutes passed. Nothing. So I put the phone back into my purse and chalked it up to a wrong number. Just as I walked toward the checkout line, I heard my phone ding, and my heart sank. I got out of line and braced myself to hear her voice again as I played the message. But it wasn't her.

It was Dorothy, her mother-in-law/neighbor who lived down the street. And her message went something like this:

"Hi Kim, it's Dorothy. I am calling to tell you your mother died yesterday. Please call me back."

I immediately called Tim. I was freaking out and wasn't sure why. He told me to call her and find out what happened. I didn't want to know, and yet my heart was hurting knowing that she had died. I walked outside and sat on the bench in front of the store. After I finally hung up with Tim, I called the number. My hands were shaking as I waited for someone to pick up the phone. After a couple of rings, a voice that sounded much older but still familiar answered.

"Hi," I said. "It's Kim. How are you, Dorothy?"

After a couple of sentences of how we both were, she told me what had happened to my mother. Mom had been on oxygen for a few years, and my brother had been living with her. She had a job washing dishes and had come home sick a couple days before Thanksgiving. She didn't have enough money to get her oxygen tanks replaced, and the last time Dorothy had gone over to check on her, my mother yelled at her and told her to leave. That was the day before Thanksgiving. Then, Thanksgiving night, Dorothy heard sirens and saw police in front of my mother's house, so she walked over and talked to them. An officer told her that my brother had called because she had died. He also told her that they found her lying on the floor in front of her chair and that it looked like she had been there for a while. Her oxygen was completely out, and her chair was full of urine and feces.

198

Dorothy told the officer that my brother had been there the entire time. She told him David must have seen Mom struggling and suffocating and didn't do anything to help. She asked if they were going to press charges, but the policeman said no. There was no proof, and it wasn't a case for the medical examiner because of her chronic illness.

As she told me what happened, I could see Mom lying on the floor as my brother walked by her to use the toilet, wondering how he could be so horrible and not do anything to help. Dorothy told me that he would go to where she worked and take her car without her knowing, forcing Mom to call Dorothy for a ride home. He stole money from Mom and lived in the house without paying any bills. She made $3.45 an hour under the table washing dishes at the local diner.

I felt horrible as she told me these things.

When she was finally done, without hesitation, I said I would come and help take care of everything. I called Tim after our conversation, my mind whirling with all I had learned. I told him we needed to go back to Kansas ASAP. Not once did I think about all of the horrible things she did and said to me. Not once did the idea of not going run through my mind. I had this weird urgency that made me plan the trip that night and leave the next day with Tim and Jessica. We drove pretty much straight through, stopping at a rest area for only a few hours. Tim was great. He drove the entire way and got us there safe and sound 19 hours later.

Once we pulled into town, we stopped and checked into our hotel. My daughter stayed there while Tim and I went to the mortuary, where my mother's body was being held. After they had gotten her out of the cooler, we were told we could go in and see her. We walked into the dark, barely lit room. Her body lay on top of a metal rack. A white sheet covered her and was pulled down to reveal her face. She looked much older than I remembered. Her thinning hair was gray, but she still had the down-turned scowl, just as she did when she was alive.

I walked up closer to see her and then turned to Tim, who was still standing in the same spot.

"Tim, this is my mom." The tears rolled down my face as I stared at her lifeless body. He walked up beside me and took my hand. He said in a quiet respectful voice, "Thank you for giving me your daughter." He took my hand and held it tightly.

I didn't speak much on our drive from the mortuary. We had arranged for cremation and paid the fees before we left. Instructions were given about what to bring to carry the ashes and when they would be ready. We left and drove to her house, where my brother still lived. The house was filthy. This was no surprise to me, but Tim was shocked at how bad it was. I walked to the spot on the floor where she had died. The carpet was stained from urine and feces. I saw the chair outside in the yard that she had sat in, and it matched the carpet, filthy and stained. David greeted us. He was sitting on the front stoop smoking a cigarette. The same stoop she would sit on years back.

"Hey, Kim. How've you been?" he asked.

What kind of crap conversation was this? I wondered.

"David, how did she die? Why didn't you call an ambulance? Were you home?" I asked all the questions at once — probably because I wasn't really expecting real answers.

True to form, he answered, "I didn't know. She was bad."

Tim, Jessica, and I spent days cleaning the house. We got a huge trailer to throw the trash in and quickly filled it. I arranged a small wake at a local restaurant, found an old picture of her in the house, and put it on a table with her urn and a bouquet of flowers. I tried to make it as nice as I could, wanting to give her a memorial where her neighbor friends could come say goodbye.

It was a small gathering, with about twelve people, including me, Tim, Jessi, and David, but it was something I had to do for her. I am not sure why, nor did I ever hesitate in doing it. I just needed to. It made me feel like I was caring for her because no one else did. I'm sure Freud would love to dissect my reaction to her death. I know I have several times, always coming to the same conclusion. I always wanted to love her, and I was always hoping she would love me back.

The day after the memorial, I told David we needed to sell the house. I didn't want to have anything to do with it, and he agreed that it was best to sell. He somehow thought he was going to get thousands of dollars from the sale, but instead, there was only $3,000 in proceeds once I paid off her second mortgage. I paid for the cremation, all of the utilities until the house was sold, and even gave him money for his medication while he stayed at the house. It sold in a few weeks, and David was sure I undersold it to rip him off. Unbelievable, but typical.

After all of his threatening and horrible phone calls accusing me of ripping him off and then begging me to send him money because he had nothing, and it was all my fault, I finally cut ties with him. To this day, I have not really spoken to him, with the exception of a call I got years later. He video-called me during work through my Facebook account. I didn't answer the first three calls, and on the fourth, I felt guilty and answered.

He had had two strokes and was in a wheelchair. His teeth were gone, and he looked 20 years older than me. He said he wanted to call to tell me how sorry he was for everything he did to me and that he felt bad. I watched as he broke down, crying and begging for my forgiveness. I had no words except, "I forgive you. Please don't call again."

I couldn't get off the call fast enough, and although he seemed to be genuine, I didn't believe a word he said. But I did forgive him. I just wanted him out of my life. I felt bad because he seemed so broken, and I always try to help people because I know what being broken feels like. But I was also protecting myself and my family from letting someone like him try to manipulate and abuse me again.

My mother's ashes came home with us and were spread among tall pines in Flagstaff the following spring. Tim and the kids came with me, but I alone walked far into the woods carrying the small urn. Once I found the right spot, an area where the sun shone through the tall pines, I spread the ashes praying to God that now she may finally have peace.

I'm not sure why I had to do this alone. Maybe I wanted to be with her for once where there was no hate, no animosity, no manipulation, and no abuse. Just her, me, and God were in that spot, and I felt like I was setting her free.

Later that year, my first granddaughter was born, and I was blessed to see her take her first breath. The love I felt the moment I saw her was so powerful, just as when I felt her mother move in my belly for the first time or when my sons were born, and just like when I was strong enough to see my tiny Julia in the NICU for the first time. I felt that same love when my other grandchildren were born, including my youngest grandson, who died because he was born prematurely. When I think of these wonderful blessings and these gifts of love, I feel sorry for my mother. Some of these moments were very hard, but they were still surrounded with love.

Love was there during the joyous times but also the bad ones. She didn't know how to receive love or give it, at least not to me. I will never know the answers to my many questions as to why she did what she did. After years of wondering, I gave up trying to figure it out because even if she had told me, I never would have understood. No answer would have ever satisfied me.

Over the next few years, the kids grew up and left to find their own paths, which was very hard for me. Since I was 18 years old, I had spent my life taking care of them, and one by one, they went their own way, discovering who they were as they did it.

I did finish everything on the list I made so many years prior. The last thing unfinished was to get a degree. Well, I did that in triplicate. I went back to school when the kids were in high school and became a respiratory therapist, wanting to give patients what I received when Julia was born. But that wasn't enough. I wanted more, so I then got my bachelor's degree in health care administration.

And after I completed that, a past professor and someone I had high respect for asked me when I would be getting my master's degree. Master's degree?!? I was shocked to get my bachelor's. My mother's voice telling me I was a mistake still lived in the attic of my mind. Earning a master's degree was something I never thought I was smart enough to accomplish. But her words stayed in my head and planted themselves. Six weeks after I graduated with my bachelor's, I enrolled myself in a master's of healthcare administration program. I worked full time and went to school online full time and earned my master's two years later.

Walking to receive my diploma in my sparkly gold high heels that I chose especially for this occasion was by far one of the proudest moments of my life. And in the audience sat the family I loved so much, cheering as they called my name. To them, I was a wife, a mom, and a Mama, and they loved me. The horrible memories of my childhood were now overshadowed by wonderful memories of this family that I loved so much. The cigarette scars may still be on my legs, but my heart didn't feel the pain anymore.

The past shaped me to be who I was, and although I didn't understand why so many bad things had happened to me, I knew that I was very lucky to be blessed with this beautiful, loving family.

Chapter 39

Through the years, I have always kept in contact with Aunt Helen. She moved to Florida after Gram passed in 2002. She was always the one who came to my rescue when my life fell apart and always the one to tell me how proud she and my uncle were of my accomplishments.

In July 2019, she and her daughter Michelle met up with Jessica and me in Colorado for a girls' weekend. This was our first girls' trip together, and I was excited — and a little nervous. My relationship with my cousin Michelle had been long-distance over the years, so in addition to seeing Aunt Helen, I was looking forward to reconnecting with some of the only family I had.

The weekend was filled with good food, a great concert, and a day trip through the mountains. The night before we were to go back home, we all sat in the den of our rented cottage and talked about family and life. We talked about my mother, and for the first time, I shared with them some details of the abuse I received from her. I told them about the cigarette burns and being left alone at seven overnight — things I had never shared before. It was only the tip of the iceberg of all I experienced. I was still hesitant to tell the whole truth.

To my surprise, however, Aunt Helen and Michelle had their own stories about my mother. Our stories were different but shared the common thread of her evil cruelty, complete disregard for the truth and others' feelings, and general abusive behaviors. We spoke about the circumstances of my conception and how I had overcome so many odds to become the person I was. "I'm so proud of you," Helen said. "You are the exception to the rule and have risen up to be an amazing mom and person."

Coming from someone who actually knew just how horrible my mother could be, this meant so much. The only other person who'd ever been proud of me was Tim, but since he had never met my mother — and didn't really want to hear the details — there was no way for him to really comprehend exactly what I'd endured and therefore, no way to know just how far I'd come.

At the end of the evening, I was about to say goodnight when Helen asked, "Have you ever thought of doing an Ancestry DNA test?" The question seemed to come from nowhere, and the idea seemed futile to me.

"My sister did one as well as my cousin," she said, referring to her older sister, my aunt Sandy and a cousin who would also be my half brother on my father's side.

"No," I said emphatically. "Then everyone will know. I don't need relatives (who see the connection in the app) to laugh and make fun of me. It's embarrassing enough to know where I came from." I told her how I imagined as a girl that my dad would come to rescue me and take me away from all the bad things my mother had done to me and how much it hurt when I knew that would never happen.

"When we were kids, Dad and I would pick your mother up at night after her beauty school class was over," she said. "But oftentimes, she wouldn't be there. She would skip class to be around guys. What could it hurt?"

You have no idea, I thought. I wasn't sure what else could hurt me more than I'd already been hurt in this life, but I knew that there was plenty of bad news to go around. I didn't need to go digging for more.

But... the seed was planted, the doubt had been sewn, and I could not unsew it. Sure enough, a couple days after I returned home, Facebook advertised an Ancestry DNA test. Two tests for the price of one. Her words kept running through my head, and that night I asked Tim what he thought about it. His reply was pretty generic and

205

nonchalant. He knew his parents, and there was no mystery about where he came from. Finally, after a week of hemming and hawing and seeing Facebook ads, I bought two kits.

During dinner that night, I told Tim that I thought we should both take the test, and that it would be interesting to see the results. I tried to be very nonchalant as I talked about how cool it would be to see where our ancestors came from and how maybe we could be related to someone famous. He listened as I rambled on.

"Kim, do you really want to do this?" he asked. "Because once you do, your results will be available to anyone who takes this test. Everyone, including your relatives, will see. Are you really okay with that?"

"Yes," I said, hoping I was convincing. I was terrified, but I had to know for sure.

"Okay," he said. "Let's do it."

Good, I thought, especially since the kits were already on their way.

They arrived two days later, and we both set up accounts, registered our individual kit numbers, spit in the containers, and shipped them back the next morning. The instructions stated that results may take up to eight weeks. We sent the test kits in the third week of July, and Tim's came back in mid-August. No big surprises for him, except he was always under the impression he was part Italian, and the DNA test didn't show any Italian at all.

Every day, I checked for my results. I got very nervous and discouraged after Tim's had come and mine didn't. I thought maybe the people who ran the test were making fun of the results. I could hear a lab tech saying, "Got another one!" And the people in the lab would laugh at the "incest family." Then one morning in the first week of September, as I was pulling out of my driveway, I heard a ding on my iWatch. It was an email alert from Ancestry.com. I immediately put the car in Park and opened the email.

"Your results are ready to view" was the subject line. Immediately, I texted Aunt Helen, who had been asking me weekly if my results had come.

"I got my results," I texted her.

"Open them," she texted back.

The first thing you see when you look at your results is your heritage. I knew that my grandfather came from Ireland, and my grandmother was half Irish and half English. When I opened my results, though, I saw that I was 50% French. I was totally confused.

"It says I'm 50% French," I texted Helen.

"What? That makes no sense... Look at your matches," she replied. Both my Gram and Papa had Irish and English heritage, with no French on either side.

The app was new to me and took a bit to figure out, especially with Helen blowing up my phone with texts. I scrolled down the matches, first seeing my other aunt listed as such, and then her daughter as my cousin, then more scrolling, and I found the cousin Helen had mentioned. If my mother had been truthful, he should have been matched as my half brother — but he wasn't — he was my first cousin, once removed.

My mind was whirling. So many of my matches were of Canadian-French heritage. Then a message popped up from a different cousin, one I had never heard of before. "Hi," she said. "Welcome to ancestry.com."

I texted Helen again to figure out what the hell is happening. "Hi," I replied to the cousin. Then I had a moment of clarity and asked her the name of her grandparents. She quickly replied. I didn't know these names at all, so I sent them to Helen, who I am sure was sitting on the edge of her sofa. Then there were a few moments of silence. I was still sitting in my car, staring at my phone, waiting for something to happen.

Helen's face showed up on my screen. She was calling. I answered, and she said, "Oh, my god. Your mother was sneaking around with a man by the name of Phil Plante. I remember going to pick her up with your grandfather from beauty school, and she wouldn't be there, but we found her a few times at the French club. He was older and doing construction up the street, and your mother would hang out with him and the neighbor girl who lived near where they were working."

My mind was spinning out of control. The DNA test proved that my cousin wasn't also my brother. It also showed that I was of French descent and am related to many French Canadians on my father's side. But most important, my mother's uncle was not my father, and I was not a product of incest!

That Aunt Helen somehow remembered this man's name was a miracle. She had been 11 at the time, with a 17-year-old sister, sneaking around with God-knows-who. Many of my newfound relatives on Ancestry.com had the same surname. It was incredible. But as I processed this newfound heritage, I remembered the last conversation I had had with my mother. She laughed at my devastation, thinking I was conceived in incest. She let me believe without any doubt this lie, and she enjoyed watching my pain when I confronted her. She knew the truth deep down inside and kept it to herself. She hated me that much.

After speaking with Helen, I drove to work, receiving a call from my cousin Michelle, who had just heard the news from her mom. Another oh-my-god moment: Michelle went to high school with Jeffrey Plante in Connecticut, Phil's son. "Everyone in Shelton knows Phil Plante," she said. He was a renowned home builder.

All of this still had not sunk in. I had to find this Phil Plante — a picture, something. At this point, I wasn't even sure if he was still alive. The relief of knowing that I wasn't a product of incest was dampened by wondering why my mother had told me that I was. She gave me a crown of thorns to wear, punishing me even after she was gone. I can't explain the toll such a thing takes a person, thinking that you are the most unspeakable mistake, worrying about becoming sick from some recessive genetic disease, accompanied by the shame of who your father was. I would never wish this dark shadow that had haunted me for the last 28 years on my worst enemy.

So after both of these conversations, and looking at my results a hundred times that day, I became the world's best sleuth. I put all my vanity and esteem aside as I searched the internet and reached out to many of the relatives on Ancestry.com, asking if anyone knew where Phil Plante was. Crickets. But then, on Facebook, I found Louis Plante, who, according to my searches, was affiliated with Phil Plante. I took a huge breath in and messaged him. It was a generic message saying that my mother had died and they had been friends, and I wanted to find him. An hour after I sent the message, he replied, "My father is Phil Plante, and he lives in Shelton, CT."

I quickly messaged back, saying that he was an old friend of my mother's and that I was trying to reach him. He didn't respond.

I wasn't giving up. Not now. I found two addresses in Shelton, CT, that were associated with a Philippe Plante. They were right next to each other, so I assumed maybe one was his business address and the other his home. I also found three phone numbers — two landlines and a cell. Both landlines were disconnected, but the cell wasn't.

I called the cell number and left a voicemail introducing myself and explaining that we shared some relatives. I gave my mother's name and the dates she lived in the area. I saved the number as "My dad." I know it sounds silly, but I had a feeling that I was on the right path. I also wrote a letter introducing myself and explaining why I was contacting him. I provided my mother's name, dates of when he hung out with her, my birthdate, and where she lived back then. And I included a picture of myself. In the letter, I only stated that we could be related, but clearly, I was indicating that could be my dad. I made sure I gave every detail I could about my mom, hoping he would remember her.

I stuffed it in an envelope, put a stamp on it, and used one of the two addresses I found. I told Tim that I planned on mailing it the next day. He was cautious and tried to talk me out of it, bringing up the negative things that could happen.

"What if he doesn't want to meet you? What about the repercussions it will have for you when he doesn't believe you're his?"

I listened to him. But my mind was made up. What if he was elated to find out he had a daughter? What if he couldn't wait to meet me? These what-ifs outweighed the negative possibilities. They were my guiding light.

I stood up for myself and said, "What's the worst possible thing that could happen? Either he accepts me, or he doesn't, but I have to take that chance."

I called Aunt Helen the next morning with my letter in my lap.

"Are you really going to do it? Put yourself out there?" She asked.

"Yes," I said. "I have to do this. This is my dad, and I want him to know about me. What's the worst that could happen? I have to do this."

I knew I was putting myself up for more rejection and abandonment, and I knew exactly what that felt like, which was exactly why I felt empowered to take a chance on the possibility of acceptance and love.

So with a deep breath and a small prayer, *Please, God. Please let this letter work,* I dropped the letter in the mailbox slot. That was on Friday, Sept 13th, 2019. I calculated how long it would take for it to reach Connecticut, and I figured it should arrive by Tuesday. In the letter, I included both my phone number and email address.

I probably checked my email that Tuesday a hundred times. And then again on Wednesday. On Thursday afternoon — almost a week after I sent the letter — I was sitting in a board meeting, and my phone vibrated. As a director of the cardiopulmonary and imaging unit, this was not uncommon. I looked at the screen to see who was calling: MY DAD. I about fell out of my chair. The meeting wasn't one I could excuse myself for, so I sat, waiting to see if there was a voicemail. No voicemail. My heart sank, but as soon as I got out of the meeting and into my office, I closed the door and called the number back.

Chapter 40

The phone rang a few times, and then a woman answered. My heart sank.

"Hi...um, someone from this number called me?" I said.

A kind voice on the other end said, "Yes, I received a call from you about a week ago, and since I am not very good with cell phones, I just noticed that I had a voicemail and wanted to return the call."

I explained to her that I found this number when I was searching online for a man who I thought could be my father. I told her his name, and she replied that she was his ex-wife, Sharon, and that she still takes care of him. She went on to explain that he had heart conditions and breathing issues, so she helps him with doctor appointments, medications, and his house. At first, I was thrilled to hear that he was still alive, but then I was scared when I heard he was suffering from conditions I saw people die from every day.

"Is he doing okay?" I asked fearfully.

"Yes, for the most part," She said. "He just needs help, and I am there for him."

I felt relieved and then told her who I was and that I had done a DNA test and believed he could be my father. To my surprise and gratitude, she didn't hang up on me. She asked me questions about the DNA test and said she was sure my father hadn't taken any. I explained the story about my second cousin welcoming me on Ancestry.com and that the last name of one of her grandparents was Plante, and how my mother was seeing Philippe Plante around the time I was conceived.

Her voice was kind and welcoming throughout our entire conversation.

"I don't feel comfortable giving you his phone number, she said. "He really doesn't know how to work it very well anyway. But I'll call him and tell him everything we spoke about and call you back. If he agrees, would you be willing to come here to meet him?"

"Oh, yes, absolutely," I said. "You have no idea how much it would mean for me to meet him."

I hung up and waited for her to call me back. I didn't quite know what to do with myself. Thankfully, I didn't have to wait too long. She called back about ten minutes later.

"I spoke with Phil and told him about your mother. And I'm sorry, but he doesn't remember her."

My heart hit the floor. *He doesn't want to see me. He doesn't remember her and probably doesn't believe a word I said.* I felt like I could vomit. I had come so far, but no further would I get. She must have noticed my silence and heard my sniffling because she said, "I wouldn't worry about that, though. He was loved by many women, and that is the reason we are no longer married. He is willing to meet you and talk if you can come." The surprise and excitement didn't stop the tears and sniffles, but now they were happy and excited tears and sniffles running down my face.

I told her I would ask my boss for time off and let her know when I could come.

Before I called Tim to let him know what had just happened, I walked into my boss's office and told her I needed to take some time off. My face was wrecked from crying, and she was surprised to see me like that. I briefly told her what had just happened, and she said, "Take whatever time you need." She was happy for me and said I deserved this.

Truth be told, I would have quit my job had she not let me go. Nothing was going to stop me from going to see my dad. I had prayed, wished, and daydreamed of this moment my entire life, and he was willing to meet me, and nothing was going to stop that from happening.

I called Tim after I spoke to my boss and told him the whole story and told him that I would go out ASAP to meet him. He brought up the practical things like the cost of plane tickets purchased last-minute and that I should take some time and plan this more, but I wasn't really listening. Instead, as we talked, I was searching for plane tickets. He knew me and how set I was and could tell he was talking to a brick wall, so he ended the conversation with, "We will decide when you get home."

I didn't leave work that day until dark. I had so many things to get done. I'd already alerted my staff and searched for flights. Everyone was so happy for me, saying I had to go and that this was a once-in-a-million chance and I deserved this.

On my drive home, I went over the phone conversation in my mind, trying to remember every word. I was listening to the radio, and all of a sudden my phone rang through my car. The navigation screen on my Jeep showed a Connecticut area code phone number calling.

"Hello?" I said, knowing but not knowing who was calling.

"Hello, Kimberly?" The man's voice sounded older, and he had a deep French accent.

I had been driving on a highway with a speed limit of 65, but as soon as I heard his voice, my speed dropped to 45 because I was so focused on his voice.

"Hi," I said.

"Do you know who this is?"

"I think this is Phil Plante?"

"I remember your mother," he said. "She was going to beauty school in Bridgeport."

"Yes, that's right!" I said. He remembered!!

"I saw her a couple years after at the mall, and she had a little girl with her. Was that you?" he asked.

"It must have been." I said. "She left when I was a baby and came back when I was three."

Then he said to me, "I am so sorry. I didn't know about you. His voice cracked as he continued. "You have my face and my eyes. You are beautiful. You got through all of those times with your mother because you are my daughter, and you are strong. You are a Plante, and I love you."

I'd waited my whole life to hear those words. I replied with words that I had longed to say for just as long – 53 years.

"I love you, too, Dad, so much."

By this time, I was going 30 miles an hour on the highway, oblivious to anything except the voice that filled my Jeep and the words that filled my heart. Nothing else mattered. I didn't want the conversation to end. I just wanted to hear his voice and feel his words, but it was late in Connecticut, and he sounded tired. Euphoria is the only word I know to describe that phone call.

When I walked into the house, Tim took one look at me and asked if I was okay. My face was splotched from crying, and I was emotionally and physically exhausted from all the beautiful things that had happened. I told him about the wonderful phone call on my way home and about the things my father said to me, and how I needed to visit him as soon as possible.

After nibbling on leftovers, I pulled up plane tickets and booked a single ticket for the following Friday, Sept 26th. Tim wanted to go, but I explained to him I had to do this on my own, that I needed time alone with my dad. He didn't agree, but he didn't argue about it.

The following seven days dragged by, but Sharon, his ex-wife, texted me and told me I was welcome to stay at Dad's house and that she could pick me up at the airport.

"Should I send you a photo so you know what I look like?" I asked.

"No need. You look just like Phil's other daughter, Diane," she said.

Apparently, I had an older sister and five other brothers. One of them, Jeffrey, had passed from suicide a few years prior. He was the one my cousin had gone to high school with. He was younger than I was.

Sharon and her son Tom picked me up at the airport. I was so nervous I could barely stand still as I rode down the escalator. She must have seen me coming because she met me at the bottom with a smile and asked me if I was Kimberly. When I answered yes, she wrapped her arms around me in a warm hug.

We drove toward Dad's house, and she told me that he was at the doctor's for a follow-up visit and was going to meet us at a diner near his house for lunch. I immediately recognized the diner and the area from my childhood. We pulled into the parking lot, and a minute later, a big, red F150 pulled in beside us.

"There he is," said Sharon. "There's your dad." I looked in the window and saw an older man, but handsome still. His hair was a salty gray, and he wore sunglasses and had a cigar in his hand.

I took a deep breath and got out of the car, watching the handsome man, who was also my dad, walk toward me. I stared at his face because there was something so familiar about it.

"There is no question, Phil. This girl looks just like you," Sharon said. He walked over and gave me a big bear hug. He was tall and handsome, and I had his face, just like he said that night when he called. Seeing him now and knowing he was my dad took away the lies my mother told me. It took away laughing at me and mocking me when she lied about who my father was. I didn't look like her side of the family. I looked like my daddy, and I finally knew where I belonged.

We went to dinner later that night, and I met my youngest brother, Jason, and his lovely wife Jen. I learned during dinner that I had actually sent the letter to Jason's house, and it was Jen who read it to my dad. They had always joked about how many unknown kids Dad had because he was such a scoundrel and liked the ladies, so no one was surprised when my letter arrived. Jason was very welcoming, but in a quiet way, kind of like Cool Hand Luke, and Jen was the exact opposite, very bubbly and talkative with an amazing smile.

There was no weirdness or hesitation from any of them. Only acceptance and kindness. I couldn't believe how at home I felt, and it was amazing. I spent time visiting with Sharon, who told me about the family, about my dad, and about life as she knew it for the past 40-plus years. I loved my time with Dad, but I could tell he needed time to process everything that was happening — and time to remember what happened 53 years ago. One day, he took me for a drive. We went past my grade school, and I learned that my older brothers had attended at the same time as I had!

Then we drove to where my mom lived when he knew her — the same home I grew up in until I was 12. On the way, we talked about her. I spoke a little of the beatings and cigarette burns. I told him that she never liked me and that I grew up in a filthy, bug-infested house. He listened to me, but I don't think he understood how bad it was — the pain I lived through, feeling like I was a mistake, and never feeling like I belonged. I broke down crying as I tried to explain how much she hated and abused me.

"You are nothing like her," he said. "Look what you have done with your life. You are *my* child."

It seemed so clear to him at that moment. I wondered if it had been just as clear to Mom. She let me believe that I was a product of incest while knowing it probably wasn't true. As she beat me, she would say, "You are just like your father," and "Your mouth and confidence will be the death of you." I know now, after meeting him, that she was referring to Phil Plante and not her uncle. She had to know who my real father was, or at least thought there was a chance that it wasn't her uncle.

Despite this unrest about my mother, my heart felt fuller than it ever had been. For the first time in my life, I felt a sense of belonging. I felt like I belonged not just with him and with this family, but on this planet, in this life. Like I was supposed to be here, to be alive. I was not a mistake. It didn't take away what I lived through, but it did make me feel like my future was going to be much different than my past. I kept thinking, *I wish you really knew me, Dad, knew my heart, me as a mom, a person.* Knowing my heritage was so very important, but I so wanted him to know *me.* I wanted to create memories with him and my new family.

On this trip, I also briefly met my oldest brother, Denis, who stopped by for a second. When he did, Dad introduced me as "your sister," but Denis thought it was a joke and didn't pay any attention to it. No big deal for me. I knew I would see him again next time, and I would feel more confident talking to him myself.

It was an amazing trip, and I dreaded leaving. I had been given my own room, and I got to kiss my dad on his forehead before I went to bed every night. All I wanted to do was stay, but I had to go home and get back to Tim, the kids, and my job. Sharon asked when I was coming back and mentioned Thanksgiving. And without consulting Tim, I asked if it would be okay if we came. "Absolutely," she said.

Chapter 41

About four weeks later, I received an alert from Ancestry.com that I had a new match in my profile. I logged in and saw the match. It was my dad. He had done the test after I had left in September. Did he not believe me? I was confused and hurt by this and turned to Tim with my questions.

"Well, it's solid evidence that he's your dad, so now no one can ever question it," he said. I decided to view the alert as a kind of birth announcement. After all, there's no denying DNA. And if my dad — or anyone else — had had any doubts before, they'd be gone now.

When I brought it up to Sharon, she confirmed this thinking, saying neither she nor my dad had any doubts that I was his child and that it was just for everyone else who may have questioned it. Tim was really great during this, providing the rational support I needed to see the whole picture.

I hadn't met my sister yet and was very nervous because she was the oldest and the only girl in the family until I showed up.

Sharon and I now texted daily, and Dad would call to see how I was doing every couple of weeks. One day Sharon told me that Dad had told Diane about me. She was the last to find out, mostly because she lived in Virginia but also, I think, because Dad was nervous about telling her. He didn't want her to be disappointed in him and his infidelity to her mom. Sharon is Dad's second ex-wife. Diane, Denis, Rick, and Jeffrey all came from his first marriage. I was born between Rick and Jeffrey. PJ and Jason are from Sharon and Dad's marriage. And Sharon had a son, Tom, from a previous marriage.

When Sharon told me this, I was excited and nervous at the same time. I could tell when Dad spoke of Diane that he had a great deal of respect for her. She was a retired Navy vet and a working nurse who lost a daughter at 30 and had another daughter who had cerebral palsy and was 35. I learned she also had a 12-year-old son who was autistic. The more I learned about my older sister, the more I wanted to know her. We seemed so similar.

A couple days after I was told that she knew about me, she sent me a text asking if we could FaceTime. Nervously, I said yes. I took a deep breath and tried to find the best lighting in the house, so I would look okay when she called.

The video conversation lasted an hour. We told each other about ourselves and talked about family. We cried and laughed, and by the end of the call, we were both in love. When we hung up again, my heart felt fuller than it had ever been, and I thanked God for these gifts. There was no other explanation for these things to be happening to me except for God answering my prayers.

After our video call, I talked to Tim about Thanksgiving and going back for another visit. He agreed to go but said we had to stay at a hotel, so he and others could have their privacy. Somehow, I procrastinated long enough in booking the hotel that there were no rooms available, and we had to stay at Dad's. I feigned disappointment.

Truth be told, I relished having my own room at my dad's. Unlike any room I'd had as a child, there were no cockroaches crawling the walls, and I felt safe when I closed my eyes to fall asleep. Even though I was an adult, I felt I had some lost time to make up for, and I didn't want to miss out on the opportunity to feel like a loved child in a home I shared with my parents — as convoluted as that may sound.

On this visit, I was able again to meet my oldest brother, Denis, and Rick, whom I had never met. Denis was loud and funny, whereas Rick was quiet and just watched me a lot. I guess everyone has their way of processing something so life-changing and weird. I also met PJ, my second youngest brother. He arrived late the night before

Thanksgiving. He was tall, and when he arrived, he ran the room. His personality was very strong and confident, and he reminded me so much of Justin that I would catch myself staring at him because their mannerisms were so similar. So far, each of my brothers was so different from one another and yet similar, if that makes sense. Somehow, I kind of just fit in. I expected to feel like the stranger in the room, but that never happened.

PJ had planned on going to a Ska concert that night and asked if I wanted to join him. Tim isn't a concert guy, but I loved live music, so I happily accepted the invite. The concert was in a small venue near Yale. We chatted about our lives in the Uber on our way there. It was very comfortable and fun. This was the first time I ever partied and got drunk with a sibling, and it was awesome. There were so many firsts happening for me in these two months, and I was in heaven. It was going to be so hard for me to leave.

As with my first visit, on the last day, Dad and Sharon asked when I would be coming back.

"Christmas!" I said, without thinking.

"We can talk about it at home," Tim said.

But before I knew it, Diane and I were texting all the time and planning what we would do during our Christmas visit. Sister things like shopping, chatting over a cup of coffee and going for a massage. We both had been planning this since our first conversation. I had to make it work. The idea of celebrating Christmas, my favorite holiday, with my dad and siblings was another first. It was the best gift I could ask for.

Somehow finding this wonderful family made me complete. I couldn't imagine my life without Tim, the kids, and the grandchildren. They are my life. But they could never fill this huge void I'd carried with me ever since I could remember. I'd been longing for a parent's love. I am forever grateful for the love and care that I received from

Gram, and had my mother not been in the picture and Gram had been able to love me like a mom, maybe this void would not have been so great.

We arrived the same day as Diane and her son and all stayed in the same hotel. The flight there was early, but with the three-hour time difference plus traffic, we didn't get to Shelton until late afternoon. We all decided to meet at the diner where I had first met Dad in September. Dad, Sharon, Jason, Jen, Tim, and I had already been seated and waited for Diane and her family to arrive. Although she and I texted and talked frequently, I was still very nervous. I didn't want her to be disappointed in me. It meant everything to me that she accepted me because I already loved her, even after such a short amount of time.

When they arrived, someone in the group said, "Diane just pulled in." I made a beeline to the bathroom.

"Okay, Kim, deep breaths," I said as I stood in the stall. "It's going to be great," I repeated. I was afraid she would resent me because of the things my mom did with Dad that hurt her and my brothers. I let a few minutes pass, thinking she would already be at the table, and walked back. Nope. She hadn't come in yet, and I was forced to sit and wait. I watched the door and saw her walk in. She was beautiful. Her eyes were bright, and her smile contagious. She looked around with purpose until she saw our group. Then she walked right up to me and gave me the biggest hug and didn't let go. We hugged and cried, and then she looked at my dad.

"Thank you for giving me the sister I have always wanted," she said to him. She hugged me again and then walked to him and said again, "Thank you, Dad. This is the best Christmas present ever."

I am sure the people in the diner were wondering what the heck was going on. Everyone in Shelton pretty much knew who our dad was; he built a majority of the homes there and even had a street named after him, but we didn't care. We laughed, ate, and shed a few tears that afternoon. It couldn't have been better, and every once in a while, I would pinch myself when no one was looking to make sure I wasn't dreaming of this wonderful family who had accepted me from Day One.

The rest of our visit was equally magical, with each day more meaningful than the one before. The day we had to leave, Diane and her crew were waiting in the lobby for us, and we followed her to Dad's, stopping for coffee on the way. When we arrived, the smell of bacon greeted us at the door, along with Red, Dad's dog, who jumped on me. Everyone was eating or waiting for more crepes, and the house had a bustling family vibe that I hated to leave. I knew I would miss it so much. I had raised my kids in the same fashion, with big family gatherings, tons of food, and everyone running around and pitching in without being asked.

I realized at that moment that all my life, I had wondered where my heart had come from. How had I always known what love was? What was right and wrong? It certainly wasn't modeled to me. As I stood in the kitchen of my newfound family, watching this warm, loving boisterous chaos, I realized my heart came from this man. Everything that was good in me — how much I cared, my work ethic, my sense of all that is right and good and pure — it all came from this man, who I am so proud to call my dad.

Epilogue

The day I left that bustling breakfast was the day I met Naomi and her husband at the airport. Our conversation in the terminal that day in December 2019 lasted two and a half hours. Our connection was so strong that I felt I had known her much longer. Our first-ever conversation that night flowed effortlessly, as did the tears. Once I had finished sharing my story, she immediately said that my story was sad and beautiful and that it needed to be shared. She had an excitement and urgency as she went on.

"Kimberly, I will help you! Although I am not an author, I have read many books and am a retired teacher. I also have a daughter who works as an editor in New York. She is brilliant, and I am sure once she reads your story, she will see that it needs to be told."

Her excitement was contagious, and I was convinced. We shared our contact information and hugs before boarding. We were on the same flight, but our seats were on opposite ends of the plane. After we landed, we met up again and made tentative plans to meet the following week. "I will call you," Naomi said as we said our final goodbyes. I replayed our conversation in my head during the flight and asked Tim as we drove home what he thought about Naomi.

"Do you think she was serious about helping me write a book?" I asked.

"Don't get your hopes up, Kim," he replied.

But it was too late. My hopes were not only up, they were sky-high. I fell asleep thinking about how my story would hopefully help others know that they were not the only ones to experience being unwanted, unloved, and unworthy of love and acceptance.

The next day Naomi texted me and asked if I would like to meet for coffee and talk more about writing this book. I jumped at the opportunity, and we made a date for a few days later. When I arrived, she was already there waiting. Beside her on the booth, she had a green fabric tote, and once I sat with my coffee, she pulled the bag up onto the table. "I know that writing this book will be difficult, but I will be with you every step of the way."

Then she reached into the bag and pulled out a large box of Kleenex. "I brought a few things you may need," she said and handed me the box. She also took out a new writing journal, Post-It notes, and finally, a bag of Dove milk chocolate "Promises" candies.

After that day, we met every week to go over my progress. I would email her the next installment the day before, so she could go over it prior to our meeting. As this book evolved, Naomi and I became so very close. Not only did we talk about the book, but about our families and lives as well. She would listen to me as I broke down on the phone after writing some of the hardest parts, and she was there for me through every step, just as she promised.

And, as she promised, she convinced her brilliant editor daughter to read this story. And like Naomi, Sarah helped with her expertise, excellent grammatical skills, and belief in my story. She helped turn it into something people would want to read and could relate to — "the next level," she called it. Naomi and Sarah were the air and water that kept me going. They never stopped believing in me, and I am forever grateful. Naomi even put together a writer's retreat for the three of us, where we spent a week among mansions, working hard to develop the storyline and edits. We shared many tears, laughs, and bottles of wine during that week. It was the best.

As many readers will have surmised by now, just three months after meeting Naomi, the world was struck by the coronavirus pandemic. As a respiratory therapist and the director of a cardiopulmonary department in Tempe, AZ, I had firsthand knowledge of just how destructive the virus was and potentially a more acute appreciation for life in general and, in particular, for my new family. I had traveled back and forth to visit every four to six weeks, but travel was restricted at the height of the pandemic.

I continued to work on my book even though doing so became increasingly difficult as I relived the pain of the past while also processing the devastation of the present. In early July 2020, I had a conversation with Tim, one that had been wearing on my heart since finding Dad. I told him that God had given me this gift, and I couldn't waste another day not getting to know my dad. He was reluctant at first, but he had seen me come home night after night broken down from the horrors I was witnessing at work. He saw the mask burns on my face and my hair that kept falling out because of stress. Finally, he took me in his arms and said, "Let's make it happen. Arizona isn't my home. You are."

We sold our home and moved to Massachusetts, which allowed me to visit Dad on the weekends and every holiday.

Although I miss my children, who live all over the United States, my beautiful home in Arizona, and my old friends, I have savored every moment with my dad. We spend weekends together in Connecticut or at his maple farm in New Hampshire. Diane and I are also very close, and we cherish our new sisterhood. My story is not over. I write new chapters with every new experience, but now those chapters are full of joy, and I write them knowing who I am, where I belong, and that, above all, I am worthy.

Acknowledgments

I want to thank Naomi Oltmanns and Sarah Anderson. If it hadn't been for you, these chapters of my life would reside only in my mind's library. Thank you to Tim, my husband, for allowing me the time and space to remember, cry, and write. To my children and grandchildren, for loving me unconditionally, and being supportive, *always*. To my Aunt Helen: Your love and memory I will forever be grateful for. To my newly found family: Thank you for accepting me with open arms. And finally to my dad: Thank you for freely giving me the unconditional love of a parent.

ABOUT THE AUTHOR

Kimberly Plante is currently an associate director of respiratory therapy at a children's hospital in Boston. She has completed many levels of education, including a master's degree in healthcare administration. Because she loves bedside patient care, she also works part time as a respiratory therapist in Fall River, Massachusetts. In her free time, she enjoys cooking, taking her three dogs for long walks, and spending time with her family.